EX LIBRIS

VINTAGE **CLASSICS**

EMMELINE PANKHURST

Emmeline Pankhurst was born in 1858 in Manchester, into a politically active family. She became interested in politics at a young age and a supporter of women's suffrage by the age of fourteen. As a teenager she attended school in Paris and on her return to Manchester she met and married Richard Pankhurst, a barrister twenty-four years her senior. Over the next ten years they had five children. Emmeline's interest in politics and involvement in the suffrage movement continued to develop and she was a member of the Women's Franchise League and later the Independent Labour Party. In 1903, frustrated by the lack of progress on securing votes for women, Pankhurst and several colleagues founded the Women's Social and Political Union (WSPU), a militant organisation devoted to securing votes for women by direct action. For the following twenty years, members of the WSPU, led by Pankhurst, endured prison and hunger strikes in their struggle to win the right to vote. Their activities were called to a halt by the start of the First World War but in 1918, the government gave voting rights to women over thirty. Emmeline died on 14 June 1928, shortly after women were granted equal voting rights with men.

EMMELINE PANKHURST

EXTRACTS FROM

My Own Story

WITH AN INTRODUCTION BY
Jess Phillips

VINTAGE

1 3 5 7 9 10 8 6 4 2

Vintage
20 Vauxhall Bridge Road,
London SW1V 2SA

Vintage Classics is part of the Penguin Random House
group of companies whose addresses can be found
at global.penguinrandomhouse.com

Introduction Copyright © Jess Phillips 2018

First published in Great Britain by Eveleigh Nash in 1914
This edition published by Vintage Classics in 2018

penguin.co.uk/vintage

A CIP catalogue record for this book is available
from the British Library

ISBN 9781784874469

Typeset in 11.5/13.75 pt Bembo
by Integra Software Services Pvt. Ltd, Pondicherry

Printed and bound by Clays Ltd, St Ives plc

Penguin Random House is committed to a sustainable future
for our business, our readers and our planet. This book is
made from Forest Stewardship Council® certified paper.

INTRODUCTION

I grew up on one of those streets where everyone knows each other. The kind that has barbeques in the summer and drinks mulled wine together in the winter. Every year one of the neighbours would volunteer to hold the street's New Year's Eve party, where the grown-ups would get howling drunk and play silly games. In 1990 my parents volunteered to have the party at our house. Being the start of a momentous new decade, it was decided that it would be fancy dress and people were asked to come dressed as 20th-century icons. Not requiring even a moment's thought, my mother knew she would be bringing in the new decade dressed as Emmeline Pankhurst.

I vividly remember sitting on the step outside my parents' bedroom as she put on her Emmeline Pankhurst costume. It consisted of a slightly flattened hat that she had probably bought for a wedding around 1983. The hat had clearly sat at the bottom layer of her wardrobe, fossilising under the weight of years of debris piling on top of it. She wrapped a scarf over the top with ties hanging down to go under her chin, pepping up the hat and lending it the air of a bonnet. Then came a plain cotton dress, with a blue buttoned overcoat, and stockings – or, in fact, pop socks, for my mother was a feminist who expressed her beliefs mainly through seeking out the most comfortable attire possible; bras and suspenders were definitely believed to be the chains of oppression. A pair of battered, black lace-up boots, which conveniently were as fashionable in the early 1990s as they had been in the 1890s, completed the outfit.

Given that the main bones of the costume were at best thrown together, she looked like a dashing bag lady (if I'm being completely honest), but the costume came alive in the accessories. My mother had made a classic 'Votes for Women' sash, resplendent in green, white and purple. She had made a 'Deeds not Words' badge, and printed out leaflets with some of the original campaign slogans of the women's suffrage movement. I was familiar with all of these additions: I had been brought up on a steady diet of women's history at home and courtesy of my childcare provider, 'The Women's Liberation Playgroup'. It was the final piece of the costume that puzzled me. It was a long coil of clear plastic hose that my dad had fashioned for her in the garage. She stepped into the spiral of clear plastic tubing, pulled it up to her waist until it lassoed her three times around her torso and finished at her shoulder where it protruded proudly with a funnel from the kitchen shoved in the end which stood to attention almost as if it was a parrot sitting on a pirate's shoulder. I was horrified by the contraption, which I felt had ruined a perfectly good costume.

'What is it, Mom?' I asked. 'It looks stupid!'

She told me that the contraption was to represent the barbaric methods that were used to force-feed Emmeline Pankhurst and her fellow suffragettes while they were in prison. She talked to me about how they weren't just genteel campaigning ladies but that they were militant women, a collective sisterhood and army. She told me she respected their work because they were fighters, who went through pain and suffering so that little girls like me could have the same rights as my brothers. She pointed at the poster on the wall in the staircase up to the attic where my brothers' bedrooms were. The poster listed all the things a man could be and still get the vote – a drunkard, a convict, a lunatic, a proprietor of white slaves – alongside the list of what a woman could be and not get the vote: a mayor, a teacher, a factory hand, a nurse, a doctor, a mother.

She explained how proud she was of these women, because of the pain and torture they endured so that I could be free. At the time the poster was one I just ran past, usually away from an angry teenage boy, but now I see how much it mattered to my mom, especially because of me, being the only girl in a house full of boys and men. I love the fact that she put it in the boys' bit of the house, knowing it was them who needed to learn the lesson most. My mom respected and wanted to pay tribute to Emmeline Pankhurst because of all she did for womankind, but she felt indebted to her, and felt love for her cause because of what her legacy offered to me, her then nine-year-old daughter.

Twenty-eight years later, on February 6 2018, I stood in a cold and cavernous Westminster Hall. It was the celebration to mark the centenary of the date when Emmeline Pankhurst finally achieved something she had fought for all her life. Votes for women. I stood there as the Member of Parliament for the seat where my mother was raised by her single mom. I stood next to Stella Creasy, the MP for Walthamstow, who was wearing a t-shirt emblazoned with the words 'Daughter of Pankhurst'. As I stood amongst hundreds of women, I cried with thanks for everything that Emmeline Pankhurst, and all daughters of Pankhurst like my mom who came after her, had done for me. These women did so much to give me power, to give me a voice, to help me to carry on the fight which was nowhere near its conclusion. That little girl, shocked by a weird funnel tube, will remain horrified for the rest of her life at what the suffragettes endured in the pursuit of freedom. A debt of gratitude like this must be repaid.

As a nine-year-old, it was Emmeline Pankhurst's deeds that I had learned about, but it was not until many years later that her words reached me. This book you are about to embark upon is surprisingly relatable and easy to read for a book written in 1914. There is a delightful mix of frustration at a need to change things coupled with what seems like a trot through thirty years of patiently chipping away at a cause. I don't know how Emmeline Pankhurst didn't give up at all the false starts. She sweeps past every time a bill was raised in the House of Commons and then fell at the first reading or somehow forgot the women bit at committee stages, as if these were just trips along the way. As someone who knows how hard it is, especially from a position of opposition, to get anything even up and running in the House of Commons, I am astounded by how temperate her language is. I know times have changed but I like to think that Mrs Pankhurst gave herself a few moments in her private chambers to eff and blind at the enormity of the task she had taken on. I would have been swearing like a sailor.

People often ask me why I got involved in politics and the answer I always give is that if anyone had seen the things I have seen when I was working with victims of domestic and sexual violence they would have the heat of rage coursing through their veins to change it. It seems Emmeline Pankhurst felt the same. I am frustrated to have to say this, but Mrs

Pankhurst's own story is one that could be told just as easily today. Her account of being a poor law guardian and the poor women of all ages that she met while she acted as an auditor of workhouses in both London and Manchester, coupled with the stories that she heard of teenage mothers abandoned and demonised while she was working in Manchester's births, deaths and marriages registration are easily comparable to the cases I saw while working in refuges, rape crisis centres and continue to see in my work as a constituency MP. While the workhouses have morphed into a gentler Welfare State, I meet women every day who are left holding the baby and feeling the shame of the absence of a man in their child's life. I regularly meet older women, whom Pankhurst gleefully describes as being far more useful and industrious than older men, who have been put out to pasture, no longer considered fit for work but without the safety net of an old age pension to fall back on as the age of qualification steadily rises. Women, as in Pankhurst's day, still bear the brunt of not only working but also taking on the lion's, the tiger's and every animal's share of the caring responsibility. This means today, as it did then, that when women reach their fifties, the years of child rearing which have lessened their wages smash headlong into the need to care for their ageing parents, leaving them with no room to earn their keep.

Alas, even Mrs Pankhurst's exclusion from joining her local constituency party of the then Independent

Labour Party in the North West, while it wouldn't happen exactly as it did then, does chime with painful similarity with some of the emails I receive from women in the Labour movement who feel that they have been discriminated against because of nothing more than their gender when trying to get involved in local committees and parochial politics.

In these modern times of intersectional feminism that seeks to ensure that all women can progress regardless of age, race, class, sexuality and disability, I have no doubt that Mrs Pankhurst – a woman who ended her life standing as the Conservative party election candidate and is often criticised for her view on the British Empire – would curry little favour. I have heard 21st-century feminists seek edgy approval discrediting her on these grounds. In the Labour movement there is no doubt that of the Pankhursts, Emmeline's rebel socialist daughter Sylvia is the favourite. By all accounts Emmeline disowned Sylvia for choosing to have a baby out of wedlock, which if we judge her by modern standards leaves us thinking that she ain't no sister. However I want to give her credit for the era she lived in, not judge her by our modern standards. The greatest intersection in the time of the Women's Social and Political Union (WSPU) was that of class, and I found this account (which is obviously written from her point of view and another view may very well be different) to tell a story of a woman breaking class boundaries. Pankhurst never seeks to romanticise the poverty of the working-class women she worked with and, even in this abridged edition, one gets glimpses of the true hero of *My Own Story* – not Emmeline herself, but rather Annie Kenney, a mill worker from Oldham. In some places it seems as if every innovative idea, and every new campaign tool that the WSPU employed, was conceived by Kenney. If Kenney were alive today, I imagine she would be General Secretary of the Trades Union Congress.

Pankhurst was as certain then as I am today that votes for women in her case, and equality for women in mine, would not simply liberate the women but in fact was and is the key to solving so many of society's problems. 'We shall have to have new laws,' she states when describing how the English Poor Law and workhouse welfare was failing so many vulnerable women, children and men, 'and it soon became apparent to me that we can never hope to get them until women have the vote.' She was not wrong. The very reason I and many other feminists have struggled to improve the agency and then the representation of women in politics is for exactly the same reason. Women don't forget women when making policy. All bar one (the 1967 Abortion Act which David Steel took through Parliament) of the greatest advancements in women's rights, education, health and economic independence were driven through the UK Parliament by female politicians. It is only now, in my era of politics, that women members of parliament and local councillors have reached the critical mass that 'women's issues' are no longer considered an add-on to the big ticket policies. It is by no means perfect, but political women from Emmeline Pankhurst to the women who sit in the Commons today force the men who make the rules to remember that we exist when they tinker with the lives of the nation.

My Own Story is an exercise in explaining and justifying the rage, anger and ultimately the frustration that led this sisterhood to arm themselves. The women of the 1960s who burned their bras and took control over their reproductive organs; the striking women in Dagenham who won for 1970s women equal pay for equal work; the 'lad culture' of the women in the 1990s sticking two fingers up to the establishment where women were in rock bands and could sleep with whomever they pleased, whenever they pleased; and in the 21st-century the #MeToo and #TimesUp campaigns which see women bleed their anger about sexual assault and harassment over every company and institution. Every action women have taken collectively since the suffrage movements of Pankhurst's day all have their locus in this shuddering rage and frustration. For a gender that is not supposed to be angry or aggressive we have spent hundreds of years kicking off. How on earth is it that women are stereotyped as meek? The underdog is always the

the old people comfortable Windsor chairs to sit in, and in a number of ways we managed to make their existence more endurable.

These, after all, were minor benefits. But it does gratify me when I look back and remember what we were able to do for the children of the Manchester workhouse. The first time I went into the place I was horrified to see little girls seven and eight years old on their knees scrubbing the cold stones of the long corridors. These little girls were clad, summer and winter, in thin cotton frocks, low in the neck and short sleeved. At night they wore nothing at all, night dresses being considered too good for paupers. The fact that bronchitis was epidemic among them most of the time had not suggested to the guardians any change in the fashion of their clothes. There was a school for the children, but the teaching was of the poorest order. They were forlorn enough, these poor innocents, when I first met them. In five years' time we had changed the face of the earth for them. We had bought land in the country and had built a cottage system home for the children, and we had established for them a modern school with trained teachers. We had even secured for them a gymnasium and a swimming-bath. I may say that I was on the building committee of the board, the only woman member.

Whatever may be urged against the English Poor Law system, I maintain that under it no stigma of pauperism need be applied to workhouse most likely to bite. Pankhurst uses this book to help people understand why she bit.

On a chilly February afternoon as the snow falls on Westminster and oh-so-British weather warnings fill the news channels, I walk from the Chamber of the House of Commons up to the committee corridor. On this journey through the members' lobby, I walk past Winston Churchill in brass looming over me, and I chuckle at the terrible write-up he gets in this book. I make my way to the central lobby where I think of Emmeline, Annie and Christabel a hundred and ten years ago, begging passing members of Parliament to choose their cause for a Private Members Bill. I swing around the corner and head to the grand spiral of stairs up to a dark and serious corridor and Lloyd George, who described Pankhurst and her suffragettes as mewing cats. Pictures of other great men pass by in my peripheral vision as I walk. Along the corridor I do not pass a single image of a woman at all, let alone a woman politician or activist, yet the men who were for so long the enemies of Mrs Pankhurst are revelled in and displayed with glory. I arrive – characteristically late – at Committee Room 16. I open the heavy wooden door from the silent dark corridor to a brilliant contrast. A big light room full of women, with a smattering of male faces. The room is so full, people are standing. Only one seat remains free, the raised seat in the centre of the crescent at the front of the room, the seat reserved for the Chair of this gathering, a cross party group here to discuss 'Women and Work – Policy Change to End Gender Discrimination in the Workforce'. The room falls silent and I take my seat as the Chair of the meeting and we proceed to try to change the world. Emmeline Pankhurst's *My Own Story* is not just her story, it is the very reason I have a story to tell at all. It is the story of why what women thought mattered. What a story it is indeed.

Jess Phillips, 2018

I

THE MAKING OF A MILITANT

I have not personally suffered from the deprivations, the bitterness and sorrow which bring so many men and women to a realisation of social injustice. My childhood was protected by love and a comfortable home. Yet, while still a very young child, I began instinctively to feel that there was something lacking, even in my own home, some false conception of family relations, some incomplete ideal.

This vague feeling of mine began to shape itself into conviction about the time my brothers and I were sent to school. The education of the English boy, then as now, was considered a much more serious matter than the education of the English boy's sister. My parents, especially my father, discussed the question of my brothers' education as a matter of real importance. My education and that of my sister were scarcely discussed at all. Of course we went to a carefully selected girls' school, but beyond the facts that the head mistress was a gentlewoman and that all the pupils were girls of my own class, nobody seemed concerned. A girl's education at that time seemed to have for its prime object the art of 'making home attractive'—presumably to migratory male relatives. It used to puzzle me to understand why I was under such a particular obligation to make home attractive to my brothers. We were on excellent terms of friendship, but it was never suggested to them as a duty that they make home attractive to me. Why not? Nobody seemed to know.

The answer to these puzzling questions came to me unexpectedly one night when I lay in my little bed waiting for sleep to overtake me. It was a custom of my father and mother to make the round of our bedrooms every night before going themselves to bed. When they entered my room that night I was still awake, but for some reason I chose to feign slumber. My father bent over me, shielding the candle flame with his big hand. I cannot know exactly what thought was in his mind as he gazed down at me, but I heard him say, somewhat sadly, 'What a pity she wasn't born a lad.'

My first hot impulse was to sit up in bed and protest that I didn't want to be a boy, but I lay still and heard my parents' footsteps pass on toward the next child's bed. I thought about my father's remark for many days afterward, but I think I never decided that I regretted my sex. However, it was made quite clear that men considered themselves superior to women, and that women apparently acquiesced in that belief.

I found this view of things difficult to reconcile with the fact that both my father and my mother were advocates of equal suffrage. I was very young when the Reform Act of 1866 was passed, but I very well remember the agitation caused by certain circumstances attending it. This Reform Act, known as the Household Franchise Bill, marked the first popular extension of the ballot in England since 1832. Under its terms, householders paying a minimum of ten pounds a year rental were given the Parliamentary vote. While it was still under discussion in the House of Commons, John Stuart Mill moved an amendment to the bill to include women householders as well as men. The amendment was defeated, but in the act as passed the word 'man,' instead of the usual 'male person,' was used. Now, under another act of Parliament it had been decided that the word 'man' always included 'woman' unless otherwise specifically stated. For example, in certain acts containing rate-paying clauses, the masculine noun and pronoun are used throughout, but the provisions apply to women rate-payers as well as to men. So when the Reform Bill with the word 'man' in it became law, many women believed that the right of suffrage had actually been bestowed upon them. A tremendous amount of discussion ensued, and the matter was finally tested by a large number of women seeking to have their names placed upon the register as voters. In my city of Manchester 3,924 women, out of a total of 4,215 possible women voters, claimed their votes, and their claim was defended in the law courts by eminent lawyers, including my future husband, Dr Pankhurst. Of course the women's claim was settled adversely in the courts, but the agitation resulted in a strengthening of the woman-suffrage agitation all over the country.

I was too young to understand the precise nature of the affair, but I shared in the general excitement. From reading newspapers aloud to my father I had developed a genuine interest in politics, and the Reform Bill presented itself to my young intelligence as something that was going to do the most wonderful good to the country.

I was fourteen years old when I went to my first suffrage meeting. Returning from school one day, I met my mother just setting out for the meeting, and I begged her to let me go along. She consented, and without stopping to lay my books down I scampered away in my mother's wake. The speeches interested and excited me, especially the address of the great Miss Lydia Becker, who was the Susan B. Anthony of the English movement, a splendid character and a truly eloquent speaker. She was the secretary of the Manchester committee, and I had learned to admire her as the editor of the *Women's Suffrage Journal*, which came to my mother every week. I left the meeting a conscious and confirmed suffragist.

I suppose I had always been an unconscious suffragist. With my temperament and my surroundings I could scarcely have been otherwise. The movement was very much alive in the early seventies, nowhere more so than in Manchester, where it was organised by a group of extraordinary men and women. Among them were Mr and Mrs Jacob Bright, who were always ready to champion the struggling cause. Mr Jacob Bright, a brother of John Bright, was for many years member of Parliament for Manchester, and to the day of his death was an active supporter of woman suffrage. Two especially gifted women, besides Miss Becker, were members of the committee. These were Mrs Alice Cliff Scatcherd and Miss Wolstentholm, now the venerable Mrs Wolstentholm-Elmy. One of the principal founders of the committee was the man whose wife, in later years, I was destined to become, Dr Richard Marsden Pankhurst.

I was between eighteen and nineteen when I finally returned from school in Paris and took my place in my father's home as a finished young lady. I sympathised with and worked for the woman-suffrage movement, and came to know Dr Pankhurst, whose work for woman suffrage had never ceased. It was Dr Pankhurst who drafted the first enfranchisement bill, known as the Women's Disabilities Removal Bill, and introduced into the

House of Commons in 1870 by Mr Jacob Bright. The bill advanced to its second reading by a majority vote of thirty-three, but it was killed in committee by Mr Gladstone's peremptory orders. Dr Pankhurst, as I have already said, with another distinguished barrister, Lord Coleridge, acted as counsel for the Manchester women, who tried in 1868 to be placed on the register as voters. He also drafted the bill giving married women absolute control over their property and earnings, a bill which became law in 1882.

My marriage with Dr Pankhurst took place in 1879.

I think we cannot be too grateful to the group of men and women who, like Dr Pankhurst, in those early days lent the weight of their honoured names to the suffrage movement in the trials of its struggling youth. These men did not wait until the movement became popular, nor did they hesitate until it was plain that women were roused to the point of revolt. They worked all their lives with those who were organising, educating, and preparing for the revolt which was one day to come. Unquestionably those pioneer men suffered in popularity for their feminist views. Some of them suffered financially, some politically. Yet they never wavered.

Dr Pankhurst did not desire that I should turn myself into a household machine. It was his firm belief that society as well as the family stands in need of women's services. So while my children were still in their cradles I was serving on the executive committee of the Women's Suffrage Society, and also on the executive board of the committee which was working to secure the Married Women's Property Act. This act having passed in 1882, I threw myself into the suffrage work with renewed energy. However, I had to go through years of public work before I acquired the experience and the wisdom to know how to wring concessions from the English Government. I had to hold public office. I had to go behind the scenes in the government schools, in the workhouses and other charitable institutions; I had to get a close-hand view of the misery and unhappiness of a man-made world, before I reached the point where I could successfully revolt against it.

Our London residence came to an end in 1893. In that year we returned to our Manchester home, and I again took up the work of the Suffrage Society. A year after my return to Manchester I became a candidate for the Board of Poor Law Guardians. Several weeks before, I had contested unsuccessfully for a place on the school board. This time, however, I was elected, heading the poll by a very large majority.

When I came into office I found that the law in our district, Chorlton, was being very harshly administered. The old board had been made up of the kind of men who are known as rate savers.

They were guardians, not of the poor but of the rates, and, as I soon discovered, not very astute guardians even of money. For instance, although the inmates were being very poorly fed, a frightful waste of food was apparent. Each inmate was given each day a certain weight of food, and bread formed so much of the ration that hardly anyone consumed all of his portion. In the farm department pigs were kept on purpose to consume this surplus of bread, and as pigs do not thrive on a solid diet of stale bread the animals fetched in the market a much lower price than properly fed farm pigs. I suggested that, instead of giving a solid weight of bread in one lump, the loaf be cut in slices and buttered with margarine, each person being allowed all that he cared to eat. The rest of the board objected, saying that our poor charges were very jealous of their rights, and would suspect in such an innovation an attempt to deprive them of a part of their ration. This was easily overcome by the suggestion that we consult the inmates before we made the change. Of course the poor people consented, and with the bread that we saved we made puddings with milk and currants, to be fed to the old people of the workhouse. These old folks I found sitting on backless forms, or benches. They had no privacy, no possessions, not even a locker. The old women were without pockets in their gowns, so they were obliged to keep any poor little treasures they had in their bosoms. Soon after I took office we gave children. If they are treated like paupers of course they will be paupers, and they will grow up paupers, permanent burdens on society; but if they are regarded merely as children under the guardianship of the state, they assume quite another character. Rich children are not pauperized by being sent to one or another of the free public schools with which England is blest. Yet a great many of those schools, now exclusively used for the education of upper middle-class boys, were founded by legacies left to educate the poor—girls as well as boys. The English Poor Law, properly administered, ought to give back to the children of the destitute what the upper classes have taken from them, a good education on a self-respecting basis.

The trouble is, as I soon perceived after taking office, the law cannot, in existing circumstances, do all the work, even for children, that it was intended to do. We shall have to have new laws, and it soon became apparent to me that we can never hope to get them until women have the vote. During the time I served on the board, and for years since then, women guardians all over the country have striven in vain to have the law reformed in order to ameliorate conditions which break the hearts of women to see, but which apparently affect men very little. I have spoken of the little girls I found scrubbing the workhouse floors. There were others at the hateful labour who aroused my keenest pity.

I found that there were pregnant women in that workhouse, scrubbing floors, doing the hardest kind of work, almost until their babies came into the world. Many of them were unmarried women, very, very young, mere girls. These poor mothers were allowed to stay in the hospital after confinement for a short two weeks. Then they had to make a choice of staying in the workhouse and earning their living by scrubbing and other work, in which case they were separated from their babies; or of taking their discharges. They could stay and be paupers, or they could leave—leave with a two-weeks-old baby in their arms, without hope, without home, without money, without anywhere to go. What became of those girls, and what became of their hapless infants? That question was at the basis of the women guardians' demand for a reform of one part of the Poor Law.

That section deals with the little children who are boarded out, not by the workhouse, but by the parents, that parent being almost always the mother. It is from that class of workhouse mothers—mostly young servant girls—which thoughtless people say all working girls ought to be; it is from that class more than from any other that cases of illegitimacy come. Those poor little servant girls, who can get out perhaps only in the evening, whose minds are not very cultivated, and who find all the sentiment of their lives in cheap novelettes, fall an easy prey to those who have designs against them. These are the people by whom the babies are mostly put out to nurse, and the mothers have to pay for their keep. Of course the babies are very badly protected. The Poor Law Guardians are supposed to protect them by appointing inspectors to visit the homes where the babies are boarded. But, under the law, if a man who ruins a girl pays down a lump sum of twenty pounds the boarding home is immune from inspection. As long as a baby-farmer takes only one child at a time, the twenty pounds being paid, the inspectors cannot inspect the house. Of course the babies die with hideous promptness, often long before the twenty pounds have been spent, and then the baby-farmers are free to solicit another victim. For years, as I have said, women have tried in vain to get that one small reform of the Poor Law, to reach and protect all illegitimate children, and to make it impossible for any rich scoundrel to escape future liability for his child because of the lump sum he has paid down. Over and over again it has been tried, but it has always failed, because the ones who really care about the thing are mere women.

I thought I had been a suffragist before I became a Poor Law Guardian, but now I began to think about the vote in women's hands not only as a right but as a desperate necessity. These poor, unprotected mothers and their babies I am sure were potent factors in my education as a militant. In fact, all the women I came in contact with in the workhouse contributed to that education. Very soon after I went on the board I saw that the class of old women who came into the workhouse were in many ways superior to the kind of old men who came into the workhouse. One could not help noticing it. They were, to begin with, more industrious. In fact it was quite touching to see their industry and patience. Old women, over sixty and seventy years of age, did most of the work of that place, most of the sewing, most of the things that kept the house clean and which supplied the inmates with clothing. I found that the old men were different. One could not get very much work out of them. They liked to stop in the oakum picking-room, where they were allowed to smoke; but as to real work, very little was done by our old men.

I began to make inquiries about these old women. I found that the majority of them were not women who had been dissolute, who had been criminal, but women who had lead perfectly respectable lives, either as wives and mothers, or as single women earning their own living. A great many were of the domestic-servant class, who had not married, who had lost their employment, and had reached a time of life when it was impossible to get more employment. It was through no fault of their own, but simply because they had never earned enough to save. The average wage of working women in England is less than two dollars a week. On this pittance it is difficult enough to keep alive, and of course it is impossible to save. Every one who knows anything about conditions under which our working women live knows that few of them can ever hope to put by enough to keep them in old age. Besides, the average working woman has to support others than herself. How can she save?

Some of our old women were married. Many of them, I found, were widows of skilled artisans who had had pensions from their unions, but the pensions had died with the men. These women, who had given up the power to work for themselves, and had devoted themselves to working for their husbands and children, were left penniless. There was nothing for them to do but to go into the workhouse. Many of them were widows of men who had served their country in the army or the navy. The men had had pensions from the government, but the pensions had died with them, and so the women were in the workhouse.

We shall not in future, I hope, find so many respectable old women in English workhouses. We have an old-age pension law now, which allows old women as well as old men the sum of five shillings a week; hardly enough to live on, but enough to enable the poor to keep their old fathers and mothers out of the workhouse without starving themselves or their children. But when I was a Poor Law Guardian there was simply nothing to do with a woman when her life of toil ceased except make a pauper of her.

I wish I had space to tell you of other tragedies of women I witnessed while I was on that board. In our out-relief department, which exists chiefly for able-bodied poor and dependent persons, I was brought into contact with widows who were struggling desperately to keep their homes and families together. The law allowed these women relief of a certain very inadequate kind, but for herself and one child it offered no relief except the workhouse. Even if the woman had a baby at her breast she was regarded, under the law, as an able-bodied man. Women, we are told, should stay at home and take care of their children. I used to astound my men colleagues by saying to them: 'When women have the vote they will see that mothers can stay at home and care for their children. You men have made it impossible for these mothers to do that.'

I am convinced that the enfranchised woman will find many ways in which to lessen, at least, the curse of poverty. Women have more practical ideas about relief, and especially of prevention of dire poverty, than men display. I was struck with this whenever I attended the District Conferences and the annual Poor Law Union Meetings. In our discussions the women showed themselves much more capable, much more resourceful, than the men. I remember two papers which I prepared and which caused considerable discussion. One of these was on the Duties of Guardians in Times of Unemployment, in which I pointed out that the government had one reserve of employment for men which could always be used. We have, on our northwest coast, a constant washing away of the fore shore. Every once in a while the question of coast reclamation comes up for discussion, but I had never heard any man suggest coast reclamation as a means of giving the unemployed relief.

In 1898 I suffered an irreparable loss in the death of my husband. His death occurred suddenly and left me with the heavy responsibility of caring for a family of children, the eldest only seventeen years of age. I resigned my place on the Board of Guardians, and was almost immediately appointed to the salaried office of registrar of births and deaths in Manchester. We have registrars of births, deaths and marriages in England, but since the act establishing the last named contains the words 'male person,' a woman may not be appointed a registrar of marriages. The head of this department of the Government is the registrar-general, with offices at Somerset House, London, where all vital statistics are returned and all records filed.

It was my duty as registrar of births and deaths to act as chief census officer of my district; I was obliged to receive all returns of births and deaths, record them, and send my books quarterly to the office of the registrar-general. My district was in a working-class quarter, and on this account I instituted evening office hours twice a week. It was touching to observe how glad the women were to have a woman registrar to go to. They used to tell me their stories, dreadful stories some of them, and all of them pathetic with that patient and uncomplaining pathos of poverty. I was shocked to be reminded over and over again of the little respect there was in the world for women and children. I have had little girls of thirteen come to my office to register the births of their babies, illegitimate, of course. In many of these cases I found that the child's own father or some near male relative was responsible for her state. There was nothing that could be done in most cases. The age of consent in England is sixteen years, but a man can always claim that he thought the girl was over sixteen. During my term of office a very young mother of an illegitimate child exposed her baby, and it died. The girl was tried for murder and was sentenced to death. This was afterwards commuted, it is true, but the unhappy child had the horrible experience of the trial and the sentence 'to be hanged by the neck, until you are dead.' The wretch who was, from the point of view of justice, the real murderer of the baby, received no punishment at all.

I needed only one more experience after this one, only one more contact with the life of my time and the position of women, to convince me that if civilisation is to advance at all in the future, it must be through the help of women, women freed of their political shackles, women with full power to work their will in society. In 1900 I was asked to stand as a candidate for the Manchester School Board. The schools were then under the old law, and the school boards were very active bodies. They administered the Elementary Education Act, bought school sites, erected buildings, employed and paid teachers. The school code and the curriculum were framed by the Board of Education, which is part of the central government. Of course this was absurd. A body of men in London could not possibly realise all the needs of boys and girls in remote parts of England. But so it was.

As a member of the school board I very soon found that the teachers, working people of the higher grade, were in exactly the same position as the working people of the lower grades. That is, the men had all the advantage. Teachers had a representative in the school board councils. Of course that representative was a man teacher, and equally of course, he gave preference to the interests of the men teachers. Men teachers received much higher salaries than the women, although many of the women, in addition to their regular class work, had to teach sewing and domestic science into the bargain. They received no extra pay for their extra work. In spite of this added burden, and in spite of the lower salaries received, I found that the women cared a great deal more about their work, and a great deal more about the children than the men. It was a winter when there was a great deal of poverty and unemployment in Manchester. I found that the women teachers were spending their slender salaries to provide regular dinners for destitute children, and were giving up their time to waiting on them and seeing that they were nourished. They said to me, quite simply: 'You see, the little things are too badly off to study their lessons. We have to feed them before we can teach them.'

Well, instead of seeing that women care more for schools and school children than men do and should therefore have more power in education, the Parliament of 1900 actually passed a law which took education in England entirely out of the hands of women. This law abolished the school board altogether and placed the administration of schools in the hands of the municipalities. Certain corporations had formerly made certain grants to technical education—Manchester had built a magnificent technical college—and now the corporations had full control of both elementary and secondary education.

The law did indeed provide that the corporations should co-opt at least one woman on their education boards. Manchester co-opted four women, and at the strong recommendation of the Labour Party, I was one of the women chosen. At their urgent solicitation I was appointed to the Committee on Technical Instruction, the one woman admitted to this committee. I learned that the Manchester Technical College, called the second best in Europe, spending thousands of pounds annually for technical training, had practically no provision for training women. Even in classes where they might easily have been admitted, bakery and confectionery classes and the like, the girls were kept out because the men's trades unions objected to their being educated for such skilled work. It was rapidly becoming clear to my mind that men regarded women as a servant class in the community, and that women were going to remain in the servant class until they lifted themselves out of it. I asked myself many times in those days what was to be done. I had joined the Labour Party, thinking that through its councils something vital might come, some such demand for the women's enfranchisement that the politicians could not possibly ignore. Nothing came.

All these years my daughters had been growing up. All their lives they had been interested in women's suffrage. Christabel and Sylvia, as little girls, had cried to be taken to meetings. They had helped in our drawing-room meetings in every way that children can help. As they grew older we used to talk together about the suffrage, and I was sometimes rather frightened by their youthful confidence in the prospect, which they considered certain, of the success of the movement. One day Christabel startled me with the remark: 'How long you women have been trying for the vote. For my part, I mean to get it.'

Was there, I reflected, any difference between trying for the vote and getting it? There is an old French proverb, 'If youth could know; if age could do.' It occurred to me that if the older suffrage workers could in some way join hands with the young, unwearied and resourceful suffragists, the movement might wake up to new life and new possibilities. After that I and my daughters together sought a way to bring about that union of young and old which would find new methods, blaze new trails. At length we thought we had found a way.

In the summer of 1902—I think it was 1902—Susan B. Anthony paid a visit to Manchester, and that visit was one of the contributory causes that led to the founding of our militant suffrage organisation, the Women's Social and Political Union. During Miss Anthony's visit my daughter Christabel, who was very deeply impressed, wrote an article for the Manchester papers on the life and works of the venerable reformer. After her departure Christabel spoke often of her, and always with sorrow and indignation that such a splendid worker for humanity was destined to die without seeing the hopes of her lifetime realised. 'It is unendurable,' declared my daughter, 'to think of another generation of women wasting their lives begging for the vote. We must not lose any more time. We must act.'

By this time the Labour Party, of which I was still a member, had returned Mr Keir Hardie to Parliament, and we decided that the first step in a campaign of action was to make the Labour Party responsible for a new suffrage bill. At a recent annual conference of the party I had moved a resolution calling upon the members to instruct their own member of Parliament to introduce a bill for the enfranchisement of women. The resolution was passed, and we determined to organise a society of women to demand immediate enfranchisement, not by means of any outworn missionary methods, but through political action.

It was in October, 1903, that I invited a number of women to my house in Nelson Street, Manchester, for purposes of organisation. We voted to call our new society the Women's Social and Political Union, partly to emphasise its democracy, and partly to define its object as political rather than propagandist. We resolved to limit our membership exclusively to women, to keep ourselves absolutely free from any party affiliation, and to be satisfied with nothing but action on our question. Deeds, not words, was to be our permanent motto.

To such a pass had the women's suffrage cause come in my country that the old leaders, who had done such fine educational work in the past, were now seemingly content with expressions of sympathy and regret on the part of hypocritical politicians. This fact was thrust upon me anew by an incident that occurred almost at the moment of the founding of the Women's Social and Political Union. In our Parliament no bill has a chance of becoming a law unless it is made a Government measure. Private members are at liberty to introduce measures of their own, but these rarely reach the second reading, or debatable stage. So much time is given to discussion of Government measures that very little time can be given to any private bills. About one day in a week is given over to consideration of private measures, to which, as we say, the Government give facilities; and since there are a limited number of weeks in a session, the members, on the opening days of Parliament, meet and draw lots to determine who shall have a place in the debates. Only these successful men have a chance to speak to their bills, and only those who have drawn early chances have any prospect of getting much discussion on their measures.

Now, the old suffragists had long since given up hope of obtaining a Government suffrage bill, but they clung to a hope that a private member's bill would some time obtain consideration. Every year, on the opening day of Parliament, the association sent a deputation of women to the House of Commons, to meet so-called friendly members and consider the position of the women's suffrage cause.

The ceremony was of a most conventional, not to say farcical character. The ladies made their speeches and the members made theirs. The ladies thanked the friendly members for their sympathy, and the members renewed their assurances that they believed in women's suffrage and would vote for it when they had an opportunity to do so. Then the deputation, a trifle sad but entirely tranquil, took its departure, and the members resumed the real business of life, which was support of their party's policies.

Such a ceremony as this I attended soon after the founding of the WSPU. Sir Charles M'Laren was the friendly member who presided over the gathering, and he did his full duty in the matter of formally endorsing the cause of women's suffrage. He assured the delegation of his deep regret, as well as the regret of numbers of his colleagues, that women so intelligent, so devoted, etc., should remain unenfranchised. Other members did likewise. The ceremonies drew to a close, but I, who had not been asked to speak, determined to add something to the occasion.

'Sir Charles M'Laren,' I began abruptly, 'has told us that numbers of his colleagues desire the success of the women's suffrage cause. Now every one of us knows that at this moment the members of the House of Commons are balloting for a place in the debates. Will Sir Charles M'Laren tell us if any member is preparing to introduce a bill for women's suffrage? Will he tell us what he and the other

24

members will pledge themselves to *do* for the reform they so warmly endorse?'

Of course, the embarrassed Sir Charles was not prepared to tell us anything of the kind, and the deputation departed in confusion and wrath. I was told that I was an interloper, an impertinent intruder. Who asked me to say anything? And what right had I to step in and ruin the good impression they had made? No one could tell how many friendly members I had alienated by my unfortunate remarks.

I went back to Manchester and with renewed energy continued the work of organising for the WSPU.

In the spring of 1904 I went to the annual conference of the Independent Labour Party, determined if possible to induce the members to prepare a suffrage bill to be laid before Parliament in the approaching session. Although I was a member of the National Administrative Council and presumably a person holding some influence in the party, I knew that my plan would be bitterly opposed by a strong minority, who held that the Labour Party should direct all its efforts toward securing universal adult suffrage for both men and women. Theoretically, of course, a Labour party could not be satisfied with anything less than universal adult suffrage, but it was clear that no such sweeping reform could be effected at that time, unless indeed the Government made it one of their measures. Besides, while a large majority of members of the House of Commons were pledged to support a bill giving women equal franchise rights with men, it was doubtful whether a majority could be relied upon to support a bill giving adult suffrage, even to men. Such a bill, even if it were a Government measure, would probably be difficult of passage.

After considerable discussion, the National Council decided to adopt the original Women's Enfranchisement Bill, drafted by Dr Pankhurst, and advanced in 1870 to its second reading in the House of Commons. The Council's decision was approved by an overwhelming majority of the conference.

The new session of Parliament, so eagerly looked forward to, met on February 13th, 1905. I went down from Manchester, and with my daughter Sylvia, then a student at the Royal College of Art, South Kensington, spent eight days in the Strangers' Lobby of the House of Commons, working for the suffrage bill. We interviewed every one of the members who had pledged themselves to support a suffrage bill when it should be introduced, but we found not one single member who would agree that his chance in the ballot, if he drew such a chance, should be given to introducing the bill. Every man had some other measure he was anxious to further. Mr Keir Hardie had previously given us his pledge, but his name, as we had feared, was not drawn in the ballot. We next set out to interview all the men whose names had been drawn, and we finally induced Mr Bamford Slack, who held the fourteenth place, to introduce our bill. The fourteenth place was not a good one, but it served, and the second reading of our bill was set down for Friday, May 12th, the second order of the day.

This being the first suffrage bill in eight years, a thrill of excitement animated not only our ranks but all the old suffrage societies. Meetings were held, and a large number of petitions circulated. When the day came for consideration on our bill, the Strangers' Lobby could not hold the enormous gathering of women of all classes, rich and poor, who flocked to the House of Commons. It was pitiful to see the look of hope and joy that shone on the faces of many of these women. We knew that our poor little measure had the very slightest chance of being passed. The bill that occupied the first order of the day was one providing that carts travelling along public roads at night should carry a light behind as well as before. We had tried to induce the promoters of this unimportant little measure to withdraw it in the interests of our bill, but they refused. We had tried also to persuade the Conservative Government to give our bill facilities for full discussion, but they also refused. So, as we fully anticipated, the promoters of the Roadway Lighting Bill were allowed to 'talk out' our bill. They did this by spinning out the debate with silly stories and foolish jokes. The members listened to the insulting performance with laughter and applause.

When news of what was happening reached the women who waited in the Strangers' Lobby, a feeling of wild excitement and indignation took possession of the throng. Seeing their temper, I felt that the moment had come for a demonstration such as no old-fashioned suffragist had ever attempted. I called upon the women to follow me outside for a meeting of protest against the Government. We swarmed out into the open, and Mrs Wolstenholm-Elmy, one of the oldest suffrage workers in England, began to speak. Instantly the police rushed into the crowd of women, pushing them about and ordering them to disperse. We moved on as far as the great statue of Richard Coeur de Lion that guards the entrance to the House of Lords, but again the police intervened. Finally the police agreed to let us hold a meeting in Broad Sanctuary, very near the gates of Westminster Abbey. Here we made speeches and adopted a resolution condemning the Government's action in allowing a small minority to talk out our bill. This was the first militant act of the WSPU. It caused comment and even some alarm, but the police contented themselves with taking our names.

The Women's Social and Political Union had been in existence two years before any opportunity was presented for work on a national scale. The autumn of 1905 brought a political situation which seemed to us to promise bright hopes for women's enfranchisement. The life of the old Parliament, dominated for nearly twenty years by the Conservative Party, was drawing to an end, and the country was on the eve of a general election in which the Liberals hoped to be returned to power. Quite naturally the Liberal candidates went to the country with perfervid promises of reform in every possible direction. They appealed to the voters to return them, as advocates and upholders of true democracy, and they promised that there should be a Government united in favour of people's rights against the powers of a privileged aristocracy.

Now repeated experiences had taught us that the only way to attain women's suffrage was to commit a Government to it. In other words, pledges of support from candidates were plainly useless. They were not worth having. The only object worth trying for was pledges from responsible leaders that the new Government would make women's suffrage a part of the official programme. We determined to address ourselves to those men who were likely to be in the Liberal Cabinet, demanding to know whether their reforms were going to include justice to women.

We laid our plans to begin this work at a great meeting to be held in Free Trade Hall, Manchester, with Sir Edward Grey as the principal speaker. We intended to get seats in the gallery, directly facing the platform and we made for the occasion a large banner with the words: 'Will the Liberal Party Give Votes for Women?' We were to let this banner down over the gallery rails at the moment when our speaker rose to put the question to Sir Edward Grey. At the last moment, however, we had to alter the plan because it was impossible to get the gallery seats we wanted. There was no way in which we could use our large banner, so, late in the afternoon on the day of the meeting, we cut out and made a small banner with the three-word inscription: 'Votes for Women.' Thus, quite accidentally, there came into existence the present slogan of the suffrage movement around the world.

Annie Kenney and my daughter Christabel were charged with the mission of questioning Sir Edward Grey. They sat quietly through the meeting, at the close of which questions were invited. Several questions were asked by men and were courteously answered. Then Annie Kenney arose and asked: 'If the Liberal Party is returned to power, will they take steps to give votes for women?' At the same time Christabel held aloft the little banner that every one in the hall might understand the nature of the question. Sir Edward Grey returned no answer to Annie's question, and the men sitting near her forced her rudely into her seat, while a steward of the meeting pressed his hat over her face. A babel of shouts, cries and catcalls sounded from all over the hall.

As soon as order was restored Christabel stood up and repeated the question: 'Will the Liberal Government, if returned, give votes to women?' Again Sir Edward Grey ignored the question, and again a perfect tumult of shouts and angry cries arose. Mr William Peacock, chief constable of Manchester, left the platform and came down to the women, asking them to write their question, which he promised to hand to the speaker. They wrote: 'Will the Liberal Government give votes to working-women? Signed, on behalf of the Women's Social and Political Union, Annie Kenney, member of the Oldham committee of the card- and blowing-room operatives.' They added a line to say that, as one of 96,000 organised women textile-workers, Annie Kenney earnestly desired an answer to the question.

Mr Peacock kept his word and handed the question to Sir Edward Grey, who read it, smiled, and passed it to the others on the platform. They also read it with smiles, but no answer to the question was made. Only one lady who was sitting on the platform tried to say something, but the chairman interrupted by asking Lord Durham to move a vote of thanks to the speaker. Mr Winston Churchill seconded the motion, Sir Edward Grey replied briefly, and the meeting began to break up. Annie Kenney stood up in her chair and cried out over the noise of shuffling feet and murmurs of conversation: 'Will the

Liberal Government give votes to women?' Then the audience became a mob. They howled, they shouted and roared, shaking their fists fiercely at the woman who dared to intrude her question into a man's meeting. Hands were lifted to drag her out of her chair, but Christabel threw one arm about her as she stood, and with the other arm warded off the mob, who struck and scratched at her until her sleeve was red with blood. Still the girls held together and shouted over and over: 'The question! The question! Answer the question!'

Six men, stewards of the meeting, seized Christabel and dragged her down the aisle, past the platform, other men following with Annie Kenney, both girls still calling for an answer to their question. On the platform the Liberal leaders sat silent and unmoved while this disgraceful scene was taking place, and the mob were shouting and shrieking from the floor.

Flung into the streets, the two girls staggered to their feet and began to address the crowds, and to tell them what had taken place in a Liberal meeting. Within five minutes they were arrested on a charge of obstruction and, in Christabel's case, of assaulting the police. Both were summonsed to appear next morning in a police court, where, after a trial which was a mere farce, Annie Kenney was sentenced to pay a fine of five shillings, with an alternative of three days in prison, and Christabel Pankhurst was given a fine of ten shillings or a jail sentence of one week.

Both girls promptly chose the prison sentence. As soon as they left the courtroom I hurried around to the room where they were waiting, and I said to my daughter: 'You have done everything you could be expected to do in this matter. I think you should let me pay your fines and take you home.' Without waiting for Annie Kenney to speak, my daughter exclaimed: 'Mother, if you pay my fine I will never go home.' Before going to the meeting she had said, 'We will get our question answered or sleep in prison tonight.' I now knew her courage remained unshaken.

Of course the affair created a tremendous sensation, not only in Manchester, where my husband had been so well known and where I had so long held public office, but all over England. The comments of the press were almost unanimously bitter. Ignoring the perfectly well-established fact that men in every political meeting ask questions and demand answers of the speakers, the newspapers treated the action of the two girls as something quite unprecedented and outrageous. They generally agreed that great leniency had been shown them. Fines and jail-sentences were too good for such unsexed creatures. 'The discipline of the nursery' would have been far more appropriate. One Birmingham paper declared that 'if any argument were required against giving ladies political status and power it had been furnished in Manchester.' Newspapers which had heretofore ignored the whole subject now hinted that while they had formerly been in favour of women's suffrage, they could no longer countenance it. The Manchester incident, it was said, had set the cause back, perhaps irrevocably.

This is how it set the cause back. Scores of people wrote to the newspapers expressing sympathy with the women. The wife of Sir Edward Grey told her friends that she considered them quite justified in the means they had taken. It was stated that Winston Churchill, nervous about his own candidacy in Manchester, visited Strangeways Gaol, where the two girls were imprisoned, and vainly begged the Governor to allow him to pay their fines. On October 20th, when the prisoners were released, they were given an immense demonstration in Free Trade Hall, the very hall from which they had been ejected the week before. The Women's Social and Political Union received a large number of new members. Above all, the question of women's suffrage became at once a live topic of comment from one end of Great Britain to the other.

We determined that from that time on the little 'Votes For Women' banners should appear wherever a prospective member of the Liberal Government rose to speak, and that there should be no more peace until the women's question was answered.

We clearly perceived that the new Government, calling themselves Liberal, were reactionary so far as women were concerned, that they were hostile to women's suffrage, and would have to be fought until they were conquered, or else driven from office.

We did not begin to fight, however, until we had given the new Government every chance to give us the pledge we wanted. Early in December the Conservative Government had gone out, and Sir Henry Campbell-Bannerman, the Liberal leader, had formed a new Cabinet. On December 21st a great meeting was held in Royal Albert Hall, London, where Sir Henry, surrounded by his Cabinet, made his first utterance as Prime Minister. Previous to the meeting we wrote to Sir Henry and asked him, in the name of the Women's Social and Political Union, whether the Liberal Government would give women the vote. We added that our representatives would be present at the meeting, and we hoped that the Prime Minister would publicly answer the question. Otherwise we should be obliged publicly to protest against his silence.

Of course Sir Henry Campbell-Bannerman returned no reply, nor did his speech contain any allusion to women's suffrage. So, at the conclusion, Annie Kenney, whom we had smuggled into the hall in disguise, whipped out her little white calico banner, and called out in her clear, sweet voice: 'Will the Liberal Government give women the vote?'

At the same moment Theresa Billington let drop from a seat directly above the platform a huge banner with the words: 'Will the Liberal Government give justice to working-women?' Just for a moment there was a gasping silence, the people waiting to see what the Cabinet Ministers would do. They did nothing. Then, in the midst of uproar and conflicting shouts, the women were seized and flung out of the hall.

This was the beginning of a campaign the like of which was never known in England, or, for that matter, in any other country. If we had been strong enough we should have opposed the election of every Liberal candidate, but being limited both in funds and in members we concentrated on one member of the Government, Mr Winston Churchill. Not that we had any animus against Mr Churchill. We chose him simply because he was the only important candidate standing for constituencies within reach of our headquarters. We attended every meeting addressed by Mr Churchill. We heckled him unmercifully; we spoiled his best points by flinging back such obvious retorts that the crowds roared with laughter. We lifted out little white banners from unexpected corners of the hall, exactly at the moment when an interruption was least desired. Sometimes our banners were torn from our hands and trodden under foot. Sometimes, again, the crowds were with us, and we actually broke up the meeting. We did not succeed in defeating Mr Churchill, but he was returned by a very small majority, the smallest of any of the Manchester Liberal candidates.

We did not confine our efforts to heckling Mr Churchill. Throughout the campaign we kept up the work of questioning Cabinet Ministers at meetings all over England and Scotland. At Sun Hall, Liverpool, addressed by the Prime Minister, nine women in succession asked the important question, and were thrown out of the hall; this in the face of the fact that Sir Campbell-Bannerman was an avowed suffragist. But we were not questioning him as to his private opinions on the suffrage; we were asking him what his Government were willing to do about suffrage. We questioned Mr Asquith in Sheffield, Mr Lloyd-George in Altrincham, Cheshire, the Prime Minister again in Glasgow, and we interrupted a great many other meetings as well. Always we were violently thrown out and insulted. Often we were painfully bruised and hurt.

What good did it do? We have often been asked that question, even by the women our actions spurred into an activity they had never before thought themselves capable of. For one thing, our heckling campaign made women's suffrage a matter of news—it had never been that before. Now the newspapers were full of us. For another thing, we woke up the old suffrage associations. During the general election various groups of non-militant suffragists came back to life and organised a gigantic manifesto in favour of action from the Liberal Government. Among others, the manifesto was signed by the Women's Co-operative Guild with nearly 21,000 members; the Women's Liberal Federation, with 76,000 members; the Scottish Women's Liberal Federation, with 15,000 members; the North-of-England Weavers' Association, with 100,000 members; the British Women's Temperance Association, with nearly 110,000 members; and the Independent Labour Party with 20,000 members. Surely it was something to have inspired all this activity.

We decided that the next step must be to carry the fight to London, and Annie Kenney was chosen to be organiser there. With only two pounds in her pocket the intrepid girl set forth on her mission. In about a fortnight I left my official work as registrar in the hands of a deputy and went down to London to see what had been accomplished. To my astonishment I found that Annie, working with my daughter Sylvia, had organised a procession of women and a demonstration to be held on the opening day of Parliament. The confident young things had actually engaged Caxton Hall, Westminster; they had had printed a large number of handbills to announce the meeting, and they were busily engaged in working up the demonstration. Mrs Drummond, who had joined the Union shortly after the imprisonment of Annie Kenney and Christabel, sent word from Manchester that she was coming to help us. She had to borrow the money for her railroad-fare, but she came, and, as ever before and since, her help was invaluable.

How we worked, distributing handbills, chalking announcements of the meeting on pavements, calling on every person we knew and on a great many more we knew only by name, canvassing from door to door!

At length the opening day of Parliament arrived. On February 19th, 1906, occurred the first suffrage procession in London. I think there were between three and four hundred women in that procession, poor working-women from the East End, for the most part, leading the way in which numberless women of every rank were afterward to follow. My eyes were misty with tears as I saw them, standing in line, holding the simple banners which my daughter Sylvia had decorated, waiting for the word of command. Of course our procession attracted a large crowd of intensely amused spectators. The police, however, made no attempt to disperse our ranks, but merely ordered us to furl our banners. There was no reason why we should not have carried banners but the fact that we were women, and therefore could be bullied. So, bannerless, the procession entered Caxton Hall. To my amazement it was filled with women, most of whom I had never seen at any suffrage gathering before.

Our meeting was most enthusiastic, and while Annie Kenney was speaking, to frequent applause, the news came to me that the King's speech (which is not the King's at all, but the formally announced Government programme for the session) had been read, and that there was in it no mention of the women's suffrage question. As Annie took her seat I arose and made this announcement, and I moved a resolution that the meeting should at once proceed to the House of Commons to urge the members to introduce a suffrage measure. The resolution was carried, and we rushed out in a body and hurried toward the Strangers' Entrance. It was pouring rain and bitterly cold, yet no one turned back, even when we learned at the entrance that for the first time in memory the doors of the House of Commons were barred to women. We sent in our cards to members who were personal friends, and some of them came out and urged our admittance. The police, however, were obdurate. They had their orders. The Liberal Government, advocates of the people's rights, had given orders that women should no longer set foot in their stronghold.

Pressure from members proved too great, and the Government relented to the extent of allowing twenty women at a time to enter the lobby. Through all the rain and cold those hundreds of women waited for hours their turn to enter. Some never got in, and for those of us who did there was small satisfaction. Not a member could be persuaded to take up our cause.

Out of the disappointment and dejection of that experience I yet reaped a richer harvest of happiness than I had ever known before. Those women had followed me to the House of Commons. They had defied the police. They were awake at last. They were prepared to do something that women had never done before—fight for themselves. Women had always fought for men, and for their children. Now they were ready to fight for their own human rights. Our militant movement was established.

II

FOUR YEARS OF PEACEFUL MILITANCY

The King opened Parliament in great state on January 29th, 1908. Again his speech omitted all mention of woman suffrage, and again the WSPU issued a call for a Women's Parliament, for February 11th, 12th and 13th. Before it was convened we heard that an excellent place in the ballot had been won by a friend of the movement, Mr Stanger, who promised to introduce a suffrage bill. February 28th was the day fixed for the second reading, and we realised that strong pressure would have to be brought to bear to prevent the bill being wrecked, as the Dickinson bill had been the previous year. Therefore, on the first day of the Women's Parliament, almost every woman present volunteered for the deputation, which was to try to carry the resolution to the Prime Minister. Led by two well-known portrait painters, the deputation left Caxton Hall and proceeded in orderly ranks, four abreast, toward the House of Commons. The crowds in the streets were enormous, thousands of sympathisers coming out to help the women, thousands of police determined that the women should not be helped, and thousands of curious spectators. When the struggle was over, fifty women were locked up in police-court cells.

The next morning, when the cases were tried, Mr Muskett, who prosecuted for the Crown, and who was perhaps a little tired of telling the Suffragettes that these scenes in the streets must cease, and then seeing them go on exactly as if he had not spoken, made a very severe and terrifying address. He told the women that this time they would be subject to the usual maximum of two months' imprisonment, with the option of a fine of five pounds, but that, in case they ever offended again, the law had worse terrors in store for them. It was proposed to revive, for the benefit of the Suffragettes, an act passed in the reign of Charles II, which dealt with 'Tumultuous Petitions, either to the Crown or Parliament.' This act provided that no person should dare to go to the King or to Parliament 'with any petition, complaint, remonstrance, declaration or other address' accompanied with a number of persons above twelve. A fine of one hundred pounds, or three months' imprisonment, might be imposed under this law. The magistrate then sentenced all but two of the women to be bound over for twelve months, or to serve six weeks in the second division. Two other women, 'old offenders,' were given one month in the third division, or lowest class. All the prisoners, except two who had very ill relatives at home, chose the prison sentence.

The next day's session of the Women's Parliament was one of intense excitement, as the women reviewed the events of the previous day, the trials, and especially the threat to revive the obsolete Act of Charles II, an act *which was passed to obstruct the progress of the Liberal Party, which came into existence under the Stuarts, and under the second Charles was fighting for its life*. It was an amazing thing that the political descendants of these men were proposing to revive the act to obstruct the advance of the women's cause, fighting for its life under George V and his Liberal Government. At least, it was evidence that the Government were baffled in their attempt to crush our movement. Christabel Pankhurst, presiding over the second session of the Women's Parliament, said: 'At last it is realised that women are fighting for freedom, as their fathers fought. If they want twelve women, aye, and more than twelve, if a hundred women are wanted to be tried under that act and sent to prison for three months, they can be found.'

I was not present at this session, nor had I been present at the first one. I was working in a by-election at South Leeds, the last of several important by-elections in great industrial centres, where our success was unquestioned, except by the Liberal press. The elections had wound up with a great procession, and a meeting of 100,000 people on Hounslet Moor.

The most wonderful enthusiasm marked that meeting. I shall never forget what splendid order the people kept, in spite of the fact that no police protection was given us; how the vast crowd parted to let our procession through; how the throngs of mill women kept up a chorus in broad Yorkshire: 'Shall us win? Shall us have the vote? We shall!' No wonder the old people shook their heads, and declared that 'there had never been owt like it.'

With those brave shouts in my ears, I hurried down to London for the concluding session of the Parliament, for I had determined that I must be the first person to challenge the Government to carry out their threat to revive the old Act of Charles II. I made a long speech to the women that day, telling them something of my experiences of the past months, and how all that I had seen and heard throughout the country had only deepened my conviction of the necessity for women's votes. 'I feel,' I concluded, 'that the time has come when I must act, and I wish to be one of those to carry our resolution to Parliament this afternoon. My experience in the country, and especially in South Leeds, has taught me things that Cabinet Ministers, who have not had that experience, do not know, and has made me feel that I must make one final attempt to see them, and to urge them to reconsider their position before some terrible disaster has occurred.'

Amid a good deal of excitement and emotion, we chose the requisite thirteen women, who were prepared to be arrested and tried under the Charles II 'Tumultuous Petitions' Act. I had not entirely recovered from an attack made upon me at Mid-Devon, and my wrenched ankle was still too sensitive to make walking anything but a painful process. Seeing me begin almost at once to limp badly, Mrs Drummond, with characteristic, blunt kindness, called to a man driving a dog-cart and asked him if he would drive me to the House of Commons. He readily agreed, and I mounted to the seat behind him, the other women forming in line behind the cart. We had not gone far when the police, who already surrounded us in great force, ordered me to dismount. Of course I obeyed and walked, or rather limped along with my companions. They would have supported me, but the police insisted that we should walk single-file. Presently I grew so faint from the pain of the ankle that I called to two of the women, who took hold of my arms and helped me on my way. This was our one act of disobedience to police orders. We moved with difficulty, for the crowd was of incredible size. All around, as far as eye could see, was the great moving, swaying, excited multitude, and surrounding us on all sides were regiments of uniformed police, foot and mounted. You might have supposed that instead of thirteen women, one of them lame, walking quietly along, the town was in the hands of an armed mob.

We had progressed as far as the entrance to Parliament Square, when two stalwart policemen suddenly grasped my arms on either side and told me that I was under arrest. My two companions, because they refused to leave me, were also arrested, and a few minutes later Annie Kenney and five other women suffered arrest. That night we were released on bail, and the next morning we were arraigned in Westminster police court for trial under the Charles II Act. But, as it turned out, the authorities, embarrassed by our readiness to test the act, announced that they had changed their minds, and would continue, for the present, to treat us as common street brawlers.

This was my first trial, and I listened, with a suspicion that my ears were playing tricks with my reason, to the most astonishing perjuries put forth by the prosecution. I heard that we had set forth from Caxton Hall with noisy shouts and songs, that we had resorted to the most riotous and vulgar behaviour, knocking off policemen's helmets, assaulting the officers right and left as we marched. Our testimony, and that of our witnesses, was ignored. When I tried to speak in my own defence, I was cut short rudely, and was told briefly that I and the others must choose between being bound over or going to prison, in the second division, for six weeks.

My first sensations when the door was locked upon me were not altogether disagreeable. I was desperately weary, for I had been working hard, perhaps a little too hard, for several strenuous months. The excitement and fatigue of the previous day, and the indignation I had suffered throughout the trial, had combined to bring me to the point of exhaustion, and I was glad to throw myself on my hard prison bed and close my eyes. But soon the relief of being alone, and with nothing to do, passed from me. Holloway Prison is a very old place, and it has the disadvantages of old places which have never known enough air and sunshine. It reeks with the odours of generations of bad ventilation, and it contrives to be at once the stuffiest and the draughtiest building I have ever been in. Soon I found myself sickening for fresh air. My head began to ache. Sleep fled. I lay all night suffering with cold, gasping for air, aching with fatigue, and painfully wide awake.

The next day I was fairly ill, but I said nothing about it. One does not expect to be comfortable in prison. As a matter of fact, one's mental suffering is so much greater than any common physical distress that the latter is almost forgotten.

Two days of solitary confinement, broken each day by an hour of silent exercise in a bitterly cold courtyard, and I was ordered to the hospital. There I thought I should be a little more comfortable. The bed was better, the food a little better, and small comforts, such as warm water for washing, were allowed.

The days passed very slowly, the nights more slowly still. Being in hospital, I was deprived of chapel, and also of work. Desperate, at last I begged the wardress for some sewing, and she kindly gave me a skirt of her own to hem, and later some coarse knitting to do.

At last the time came when they gave me back all my things, and let me go free. At the door the Governor spoke to me, and asked me if I had any complaints to make. 'Not of you,' I replied, 'nor of any of the wardresses. Only of this prison, and all of men's prisons. We shall raze them to the ground.'

Back in my comfortable home, surrounded by loving friends, I would have rested quietly for a few days, but there was a great meeting that night at Albert Hall, to mark the close of a week of self-denial to raise money for the year's campaign. Women had sold papers, flowers, toys, swept crossings, and sung in the streets for the cause. Many women, well known in the world of art and letters, did these things. I felt that I should be doing little if I merely attended the meeting. So I went. My release was not expected until the following morning, and no one thought of my appearing at the meeting. My chairman's seat was decorated with a large placard with the inscription, 'Mrs Pankhurst's Chair.' After all the others were seated, the speakers, and hundreds of ex-prisoners, I walked quietly onto the stage, took the placard out of the chair and sat down. A great cry went up from the women as they sprang from their seats and stretched their hands toward me. It was some time before I could see them for my tears, or speak to them for the emotion that shook me like a storm.

The next morning I, with the other released prisoners, drove off to Peckham, a constituency of London, where the WSPU members were fighting a vigorous by-election. In open brakes we paraded the streets, dressed in our prison clothes, or exact reproductions of them. Naturally, we attracted a great deal of attention and sympathy, and our daily meetings on Peckham Rye, as their common is known, drew enormous crowds. When polling day came our members were stationed at every polling booth, and many men as they came to the booths told us that they were, for the first time, voting 'for the women,' by which they meant against the Government. That night, amid great excitement, it was made known that the Liberal majority of 2,339 at the last general election had been turned into a Conservative majority of 2,494. Letters poured into the newspapers, declaring that the loss of this important Liberal seat was due almost entirely to the work of the Suffragettes, and many prominent Liberals called upon party leaders to start doing something for women before the next general election. The Liberal leaders, with the usual perspicacity of politicians, responded not at all. Instead they beheld with approval the rise to highest power the arch-enemy of the suffragists, Mr Asquith.

Mr Asquith became Prime Minister about Easter time, 1908, on the resignation, on account of ill health, of Sir Henry Campbell-Bannerman. Mr Asquith was chosen, not because of any remarkable record of statesmanship, nor yet because of great personal popularity—for he possessed neither—but simply because no better man seemed available just then. He was known as a clever, astute, and somewhat unscrupulous politician. He had filled several high offices to the satisfaction of his party, and under Sir Henry Campbell-Bannerman had been Chancellor of the Exchequer, a post which is generally regarded as a stepping-stone to the Premiership. The best thing the Liberal press found to say of the new Premier was that he was a 'strong' man. Generally in politics this term is used to describe an obstinate man, and this we already knew Mr Asquith to be. He was a bluntly outspoken opponent of woman suffrage, and it was sufficiently plain to us that no methods of education or persuasion would ever prove successful where he was concerned. Therefore the necessity of action on our part was greater than ever.

The year 1910 began with a general election, precipitated by the House of Lords' rejection of Mr Lloyd-George's 1909 budget. The Liberal Party went to the country with promises of taxes on land values. They promised also abolition of the veto power of the Lords, Irish Home Rule, disestablishment of the

Church of Wales, and other reforms. Woman suffrage was not directly promised, but Mr Asquith pledged that, if retained in office, he would introduce an electoral reform bill which could be amended to include woman suffrage. The Unionists under the leadership of Mr Balfour, had tariff reform for their programme, and they offered not even a vague promise of a possible suffrage measure. Yet we, as usual, went into the constituencies and opposed the Liberal Party. We had no faith in Mr Asquith's pledge, and besides, if we had failed to oppose the party in power we should but have invited Mr Asquith and Mr Balfour to enter into an agreement not to deal with the suffrage, with the view of keeping the cause permanently outside practical politics.

We opposed Liberal candidates in forty constituencies, and in almost every one of these the Liberal majorities were reduced and no less than eighteen seats were wrested from the Liberal candidates. It really was a terrible election for the Government. Mr Asquith travelled from one constituency to another accompanied by a bodyguard of detectives, and official 'chuckers out,' whose sole duty was to eject women, and men as well, who interrupted his meetings on the question of Votes for Women. The halls where he spoke had the windows boarded up or the glass covered with strong wire netting. Every thoroughfare leading to the halls was barricaded, traffic was suspended, and large forces of police were on guard. The most extraordinary precautions were taken to protect the Prime Minister. At one place he went to his meeting strongly guarded and by way of a secret pathway that led through gooseberry bushes and a cabbage patch to a back door. After the meeting he escaped through the same door and was solemnly guided along a path heavily laid with sawdust to deaden his footsteps, to a concealed motor car, where he sat until the crowd had all dispersed.

The other ministers had to resort to similar precautions. They lived under the constant protection of bodyguards. Their meetings were policed in a manner without precedent. Of course no women were admitted to their meetings, but they got in just the same. Two women hid for twenty-five hours in the rafters of a hall in Louth where Mr Lloyd-George spoke. They were arrested, but not until after they had made their demonstration. Two others hid under a platform for twenty-two hours in order to question the Prime Minister. I could continue this record almost indefinitely.

The Liberal Party was returned to power, but with their majority over all sections of the House of Commons swept away. The Asquith Government were dependent now for their very existence on the votes of the Labour Party and the Irish Nationalists.

The first months of 1910 were occupied by the re-elected Government in a struggle to keep control of affairs. A coalition with the Irish party, the leaders of which agreed, if the Home Rule bill were advanced, to stand by the budget. No publicly announced coalition with the Labour Party was made at that time, Keir Hardie, at the annual conference of the party, announcing that they would continue to be independent of the Government. This was important to us because it meant that the Labour Party, instead of entering into an agreement to give general support to all Government measures, would be free to oppose the Government in the event of the continued withholding of a franchise bill. Other things combined to make us hopeful that the tide had turned in our favour. It was hinted to us that the Government were weary of our opposition and were ready to end the struggle in the only possible way, providing they could do so without appearing to yield to coercion. We therefore, early in February, declared a truce to all militancy.

Parliament met on February 15th and the King's speech was read on February 21st. No mention of women's suffrage was made in the speech nor was any private member successful in winning a place in the ballot for a suffrage bill. However, since the situation, on account of the proposed abolition of the Lords' power of veto, was strained and abnormal, we decided to wait patiently for a while. It was confidently expected that another general election would have to be held before the contentions between the two Houses of Parliament were settled, and this event unquestionably would have occurred, not later than June, but for the unexpected death of King Edward VII. This interrupted the strained situation. The passing of the King served as an occasion for the temporary softening of animosities and produced a general disposition to compromise on all troubled issues. The question of women's enfranchisement was taken up again in this spirit, and in a manner altogether creditable to the members with whom the movement originated.

A strictly non-party committee on women's suffrage had been established in the House of Commons in 1887, mainly through the efforts of Miss Lydia Becker. In 1906, for reasons not necessary to enumerate, the original committee had been allowed to lapse, the Liberal supporters of women's suffrage forming a committee of their own. Now, in this period of good feeling, at the suggestion of certain members, led by Mr H. N. Brailsford, not himself a member of Parliament, formed another non-party body which they called the Conciliation Committee. Its object was declared to be the bringing together of the full strength of suffragists of the House of Commons, regardless of party affiliation, and of framing a suffrage measure that could be passed by their united effort. The Earl of Lytton accepted the chairmanship of the committee and Mr Brailsford was made its secretary. The committee consisted of twenty-five Liberals, seventeen Conservatives, six Irish Nationalists, and six members of the Labour Party. Under difficulties the committee laboured to frame a bill which should win the support of all sections of the House. The Conservatives insisted on a moderate bill, whilst the Liberals were concerned lest the terms of the bill should add to the power of the propertied classes. The original suffrage bill, drafted by my husband, Dr Pankhurst, giving the vote to women on equal terms with men, was abandoned, and a bill was drawn up along the lines of the existing municipal franchise law. The basis of the municipal franchise is occupation, and the Conciliation Bill, as first drafted, proposed to extend the Parliamentary vote to women householders, and to women occupiers of business premises paying ten pounds rental and upwards. It was estimated that about ninety-five per cent of the women who would be enfranchised under the bill were householders. This, in England, does not mean a person occupying a whole house. Any one who inhabits even a single room over which he or she exercises full control is a householder.

The text of the Conciliation Bill was submitted to all the suffrage societies and other women's organisations, and it was accepted by every one of them. Our official newspaper said editorially: 'We of the Women's Social and Political Union are prepared to share in this united and peaceful action. The new bill does not give us all that we want, but we are for it if others are also for it.'

It seemed certain that an overwhelming majority of the House of Commons were for the bill, and were prepared to vote it into law. Although we knew that it could not possibly pass unless the Government agreed that it should, we hoped that the leaders of all parties and the majority of their followers would unite in an agreement that the bill should pass. This settlement by consent is rare in the English Parliament, but some extremely important and hard fought measures have been carried thus. The extension of the franchise in 1867 is a case in point.

The Conciliation Bill was introduced into the House of Commons on June 14th, 1910, by Mr D. J. Shackleton, and was received with the most extraordinary enthusiasm. The newspapers remarked on the feeling of reality which marked the attitude of the House towards the bill. It was plain that the members realised that here was no academic question upon which they were merely to debate and to register their opinions, but a measure which was intended to be carried through all its stages and to be written into English law. The enthusiasm of the House swept all over the Kingdom. The medical profession sent in a memorial in its favour, signed by more than three hundred of the most distinguished men and women in the profession. Memorials from writers, clergymen, social workers, artists, actors, musicians, were also sent. The Women's Liberal Federation met and unanimously resolved to ask the Prime Minister to give full facilities to the bill. Some advanced spirits in the Federation actually proposed to send then and there a deputation to the House of Commons with the resolution, but this proposal was rejected as savouring too much of militancy. A request for an interview was sent to Mr Asquith, and he replied promising to receive, at an early day, representatives of both the Liberal Women's Federation and of the National Union of Women's Suffrage Societies.

The joint deputation was received by Mr Asquith on June 21st, and Lady M'Laren, as a representative of the Women's Liberal Federation, spoke very directly to her party's leader. She said in part: 'If you refuse our request we shall have to go to the country and say you, who are against the veto of the House of Lords, are placing a veto on the House of Commons by refusing to allow a second reading of this bill.'

Mr Asquith replied warily that he could not decide alone on such a serious matter, but would have to consult his Cabinet, the majority of whom, he admitted, were suffragists. Their decision, he said, would be given in the House of Commons.

The Women's Social and Political Union arranged a demonstration in support of the Conciliation Bill, the greatest that had, up to that time, been made. It was a national, indeed an inter-national affair in which all the suffrage groups took part, and its massed ranks were so great that the procession required an hour and a half to pass a given point. At the head marched six hundred and seventeen women, white clad and holding long silver staves tipped with the broad arrow. These were the women who had suffered imprisonment for the cause, and all along the line of march they received a tribute of cheers from the public. The immense Albert Hall, the largest hall in England, although it was packed from orchestra to the highest gallery, was not large enough to hold all the marchers. Amid great joy and enthusiasm Lord Lytton delivered a stirring address in which he confidently predicted the speedy advance of the bill. The women, he declared, had every reason to believe that their enfranchisement was actually at hand.

It was true that the time for passing a suffrage bill was ripe. Not in fifty years had the way been so clear, because the momentary absence of ordinary legislation left the field open for an electoral reform bill. Yet when the Prime Minister was asked in the House of Commons whether he would give the members an early opportunity for discussion, the answer was not encouraging. The Government, said Mr Asquith, were prepared to give time before the close of the session for full debate and division on second reading, but they could not allow any further facilities. He stated frankly that he personally did not want the bill to pass, but the Government realised that the House of Commons ought to have an opportunity, if that was their deliberate desire, for effectively dealing with the whole question.

This cryptic utterance was taken by the majority of the suffragists, by the press and by the public generally to mean that the Government were preparing gracefully to yield to the undoubted desire of the House of Commons to pass the bill. But the Women's Social and Political Union were doubtful. Mr Asquith's remark was ambiguous, and was capable of being interpreted in several ways. It could mean that he was prepared to accept the verdict of the majority and let the bill pass through all its stages. That of course would be the only way to allow the House opportunity effectively to deal with the whole question. On the other hand Mr Asquith might be intending to let the bill pass through its debating stages and be afterwards smothered in committee. We feared treachery, but in view of the announcement that the Government had set apart July 11th and 12th for debate on the second reading, we preserved a spirit of waiting calm. July 26th had been fixed as the day for the adjournment of Parliament, and if the bill was voted on favourably on the 12th there would be ample time to take it through its final stages.

Some days before the bill reached its second reading it was rumoured that Mr Lloyd-George was going to speak against it, but we refused to credit this. Unfair to women as Mr Lloyd-George had shown himself in various ways, he had consistently posed as a staunch friend of women's suffrage, and we could not believe that he would turn against us at the eleventh hour. Mr Winston Churchill, the promoters of the bill also counted upon, as it was known that he had more than once expressed sympathy with its objects. But when the debates began we found both of these ardent suffragists arrayed against the bill. Mr Churchill, after making a conventional anti-suffrage speech, in which he said that women did not need the ballot, and that they really had no grievances, attacked the Conciliation Bill because the class of women who would be enfranchised under it did not suit him. Some women, he conceded, ought to be enfranchised, and he thought the best plan would be to select 'some of the best women of all classes' on considerations of property, education and earning capacity. These special franchises would be carefully balanced, 'so as not on the whole to give undue advantage to the property vote against the wage earning vote.' A more fantastic proposal and one less likely to find favour in the House of Commons could not possibly be imagined. Mr Churchill's second objection to the bill was that it was anti-democratic! It seemed to us that anything was more democratic than his proposed 'fancy' franchises.

Mr Lloyd-George said that he agreed with everything Mr Churchill had said 'both relevant and irrelevant.' He made the amazing assertion that the Conciliation Committee that had drafted the bill was a 'committee of women meeting outside the House.' And that this committee said to the House of Commons not only that they must vote for a women's suffrage bill but 'You must vote for the particular form upon which we agree, and we will not even allow you to deliberate upon any other form.'

Of course these statements were wholly false. The Conciliation Bill was drafted by men, and it was introduced because the Government had refused to bring in a party measure. The suffragists would have been only too glad to have had the Government deliberate on a broader form of suffrage. Because they refused to deliberate on any form, this private bill was introduced.

This fact was brought forward in the course of Mr Lloyd-George's speech. It had been urged, said he, that this bill was better than none at all, but why should that be the alternative? 'What is the other?' called out a member, but Mr Lloyd-George dodged the question with a careless 'Well, I cannot say for the present.'

Later on he said: 'If the promoters of this bill say that they regard the second reading merely as an affirmation of the principle of women's suffrage, and if they promise that when they re-introduce the bill it will be in a form which will enable the House of Commons to move any amendment either for restriction or extension I shall be happy to vote for this bill.'

Mr Philip Snowden, replying to this, said: 'We will withdraw this bill if the Right Honourable gentleman, on behalf of the Government, or the Prime Minister himself will undertake to give to this House the opportunity of discussing and carrying through its various stages another form of franchise bill. If we cannot get that, then we shall prosecute this bill.'

The Government made no reply at all to this, and the debate proceeded. Thirty-nine speeches were made, the Prime Minister showing plainly in his speech that he intended to use all his power to prevent the bill becoming law. He began by saying that a franchise measure ought never to be sent to a Grand Committee, but to one of the Whole House. He said also that his conditions, that the majority of women should show beyond any doubt that they desired the franchise, and that the bill be democratic in its terms, had not been complied with.

When the division was taken it was seen that the Conciliation Bill had passed its second reading by a majority of 109, a larger majority than the Government's far famed budget or the House of Lords Resolution had received. In fact no measure during that Parliament had received so great a majority—299 members voted for it as against 190 opposed. Then the question arose as to which committee should deal with the bill. Mr Asquith had said that all franchise bills should go to a

Committee of the Whole House, so that in the division his words moved many sincere friends of the bill to send it there. Others understood that this was a mischievous course, but were afraid of incurring the anger of the Prime Minister. Of course all the anti-suffragists voted the same way, and thus the bill went to the Whole House.

Even then the bill could have been advanced to its final reading. The House had time on their hands, as virtually all important legislative work was halted because of the deadlock between the Lords and the Commons. Following the death of the King a conference of leaders of the Conservative and the Liberal Parties had been arranged to adjust the matters at issue, and this conference had not yet reported. Hence Parliament had little business on hand. The strongest possible pressure was brought to bear upon the Government to give facilities to the Conciliation Bill. A number of meetings were held in support of the bill. The Men's Political Union for Women's Enfranchisement, the Men's League for Women's Suffrage and the Conciliation Committee held a joint meeting in Hyde Park. Some of the old school of suffragists held another large meeting in Trafalgar Square. The Women's Social and Political Union, on July 23rd, which was the anniversary of the day in 1867 on which working men, agitating for their vote, had pulled down the Hyde Park railings, held another enormous demonstration there. A space of half a square mile was cleared, forty platforms erected, and two great processions marched from east and west to the meeting. Many other suffrage societies co-operated with us on this occasion. On the very day of that meeting Mr Asquith wrote to Lord Lytton refusing to allow any more time for the bill during that session.

It had been exceedingly difficult, during these troublous days, to hold all the members of the WSPU to the truce, and when it became perfectly apparent that the Conciliation Bill was doomed, war was again declared. At a great meeting held in Albert Hall on November 10th, I myself threw down the gage of battle. I said, because I wanted the whole matter to be clearly understood by the public as well as by our members: 'This is the last constitutional effort of the Women's Social and Political Union to secure the passage of the bill into law. If the bill, in spite of our efforts, is killed by the Government, then first of all, I have to say there is an end of the truce. If we are met by the statement that there is no power to secure on the floor of the House of Commons time for our measure, then our first step is to say, "We take it out of your hands, since you fail to help us, and we resume the direction of the campaign ourselves."'

Another deputation, I declared, must go to the House of Commons to carry a petition to the Prime Minister. I myself would lead, and if no one cared to follow me I would go alone. Instantly, all over the hall, women sprang to their feet crying out, 'Mrs Pankhurst, I will go with you!' 'I will go!' 'I will go!' And I knew that our brave women were as ever ready to give themselves, their very lives, if need be, for the cause of freedom.

The autumn session convened on Friday, November 18th, and Mr Asquith announced that Parliament would be adjourned on November 28th. While his speech was in progress, 450 women, in small groups, to keep within the strict letter of the law, were marching from Caxton Hall and from the headquarters of the Union.

How to tell the story of that dreadful day, Black Friday, as it lives in our memory—how to describe what happened to English women at the behest of an English Government, is a difficult task. I will try to tell it as simply and as accurately as possible. The plain facts, baldly stated, I am aware will strain credulity.

Remember that the country was on the eve of a general election, and that the Liberal Party needed the help of Liberal women. This fact made the wholesale arrest and imprisonment of great numbers of women, who were demanding the passage of the Conciliation Bill, extremely undesirable from the Government's point of view. The Women's Liberal Federation also wanted the passage of the Conciliation Bill, although they were not ready to fight for it. What the Government feared, was that the Liberal women would be stirred by our sufferings into refraining from doing election work for the party. So the Government conceived a plan whereby the Suffragettes were to be punished, were to be turned back and defeated in their purpose of reaching the House, but would not be arrested. Orders were evidently given that the police were to be present in the streets, and that the women were to be thrown from one uniformed or ununiformed policeman to another, that they were to be so rudely treated that sheer terror would cause them to turn back. I say orders were given and as one proof of this I can first point out that on all previous occasions the police had first tried to turn back the deputations and when the women persisted in going forward, had arrested them. At times individual policemen had behaved with cruelty and malice toward us, but never anything like the unanimous and wholesale brutality that was shown on Black Friday.

The Government very likely hoped that the violence of the police towards the women would be emulated by the crowds, but instead the crowds proved remarkably friendly. They pushed and struggled to make a clear pathway for us, and in spite of the efforts of the police my small deputation actually succeeded in reaching the door of the Strangers' Entrance. We mounted the steps to the enthusiastic cheers of the multitudes that filled the streets, and we stood there for hours gazing down on a scene which I hope never to look upon again.

At intervals of two or three minutes small groups of women appeared in the square, trying to join us at the Strangers' Entrance. They carried little banners inscribed with various mottoes, 'Asquith Has Vetoed Our Bill,' 'Where There's a Bill There's a Way,' 'Women's Will Beats Asquith's Won't,' and the like. These banners the police seized and tore in pieces. Then they laid hands on the women and literally threw them from one man to another. Some of the police used their fists, striking the women in their faces, their breasts, their shoulders. One woman I saw thrown down with violence three or four times in rapid succession, until at last she lay only half conscious against the curb, and in a serious condition was carried away by kindly strangers. Every moment the struggle grew fiercer, as more and more women arrived on the scene. Women, many of them eminent in art, in medicine and science, women of European reputation, subjected to treatment that would not have been meted out to criminals, and all for the offence of insisting upon the right of peaceful petition.

This struggle lasted for about an hour, more and more women successfully pushing their way past the police and gaining the steps of the House. Then the mounted police were summoned to turn the women back. But, desperately determined, the women, fearing not the hoofs of the horses or the crushing violence of the police, did not swerve from their purpose. And now the crowds began to murmur.

People began to demand why the women were being knocked about; why, if they were breaking the law, they were not arrested; why, if they were not breaking the law, they were not permitted to go on unmolested. For a long time, nearly five hours, the police continued to hustle and beat the women, the crowds becoming more and more turbulent in their defence. Then, at last the police were obliged to make arrests. One hundred and fifteen women and four men, most of them bruised and choked and otherwise injured, were arrested.

While all this was going on outside the House of Commons, the Prime Minister was obstinately refusing to listen to the counsels of some of the saner and more justice-loving members of the House. Keir Hardie, Sir Alfred Mondell and others urged Mr Asquith to receive the deputation, and Lord Castlereagh went so far as to move as an amendment to a Government proposal, another proposal which would have compelled the Government to provide immediate facilities to the Conciliation Bill. We heard of what was going on, and I sent in for one and another friendly member and made every possible effort to influence them in favour of Lord Castlereagh's amendment. I pointed to the brutal struggle that was going on in the square, and I begged them to go back and tell the others that it must be stopped. But, distressed as some of them undoubtedly were, they assured me that there was not the slightest chance for the amendment.

'Is there not a single *man* in the House of Commons,' I cried, 'one who will stand up for us, who will make the House see that the amendment must go forward?'

Well, perhaps there were men there, but all save fifty-two put their party loyalty before their manhood, and, because Lord Castlereagh's proposal would have meant censure of the Government, they refused to support it. This did not happen, however, until Mr Asquith had resorted to his usual crafty device of a promise of future action. In this instance he promised to make a statement on behalf of the Government on the following Tuesday.

The next morning the suffrage prisoners were arraigned in police court. Or rather, they were kept waiting outside the courtroom while Mr Muskett, who prosecuted on behalf of the Chief Commissioner of Police, explained to the astounded magistrate that he had received orders from the Home Secretary that the prisoners should all be discharged. Mr Churchill it was declared, had had the matter under careful consideration, and had decided that 'no public advantage would be gained by proceeding with the prosecution, and accordingly no evidence would be given against the prisoners.'

On the following Tuesday the WSPU held another meeting of the Women's Parliament in Caxton Hall to hear the news from the House of Commons. Mr Asquith said: 'The Government will, if they are still in power, give facilities in the next Parliament for effectively proceeding with a franchise bill which is so framed as to admit of free amendment.' He would not promise that this would be done during the first year of Parliament.

We had demanded facilities for the Conciliation Bill, and Mr Asquith's promise was too vague and too ambiguous to please us. The Parliament now about to be dissolved had lasted a scant ten months. The next one might not last longer. Therefore, Mr Asquith's promise, as usual, meant nothing at all. I said to the women, 'I am going to Downing Street. Come along, all of you.' And we went.

We found a small force of police in Downing Street, and we easily broke through their line and would have invaded the Prime Minister's residence had not reinforcements of police arrived on the scene. Mr Asquith himself appeared unexpectedly, and as we thought, very opportunely. Before he could have realised what was happening he found himself surrounded by angry Suffragettes. He was well hooted and, it is said, well shaken, before he was rescued by the police. As his taxicab rushed away some object struck one of the windows, smashing it.

Another Cabinet Minister, Mr Birrell, unwittingly got into the midst of the mêlée, and I am obliged to record that he was pretty thoroughly hustled. But it is not true that his leg was injured by the women. His haste to jump into a taxicab resulted in a slightly sprained ankle.

That night and the following day windows were broken in the houses of Sir Edward Grey, Mr Winston Churchill, Mr Lewis Harcourt and Mr John Burns; and also in the official residences of the Premier and the Chancellor of the Exchequer.

That week 160 Suffragettes were arrested, but all except those charged with window-breaking or assault were discharged. This amazing court action established two things: First, that when the Home Secretary stated that he had no responsibility for the prosecution and sentencing of suffrage prisoners, he told a colossal falsehood; and second, that the Government fully realised that it was bad election tactics to be responsible for the imprisonment of women of good character who were struggling for citizenship.

III

THE WOMEN'S REVOLUTION

On February 16th we held a large meeting of welcome to a number of released prisoners who had served two and three months for the window-breaking demonstration that had taken place in the previous November. At this meeting we candidly surveyed the situation and agreed on a course of action which we believed would be sufficiently strong to prevent the Government from advancing their threatened franchise bill. I said on this occasion:

'We don't want to use any weapons that are unnecessarily strong. If the argument of the stone, that time-honoured official political argument, is sufficient, then we will never use any stronger argument. And that is the weapon and the argument that we are going to use next time. And so I say to every volunteer on our demonstration, "Be prepared to use that argument." I am taking charge of the demonstration, and that is the argument I am going to use. I am not going to use it for any sentimental reason, I am going to use it because it is the easiest and the most readily understood. Why should women go to Parliament Square and be battered about and insulted, and most important of all, produce less effect than when they throw stones? We tried it long enough. We submitted for years patiently to insult and assault. Women had their health injured. Women lost their lives. We should not have minded if that had succeeded, but that did not succeed, and we have made more progress with less hurt to ourselves by breaking glass than ever we made when we allowed them to break our bodies.

'After all, is not a woman's life, is not her health, are not her limbs more valuable than panes of glass? There is no doubt of that, but most important of all, does not the breaking of glass produce more effect upon the Government? If you are fighting a battle, that should dictate your choice of weapons. Well, then, we are going to try this time if mere stones will do it. I do not think it will ever be necessary for us to arm ourselves as Chinese women have done, but there are women who are prepared to do that if it should be necessary. In this Union we don't lose our heads. We only go as far as we are obliged to go in order to win, and we are going forward with this next protest demonstration in full faith that this plan of campaign, initiated by our friends whom we honour tonight, will on this next occasion prove effective.'

Ever since militancy took on the form of destruction of property the public generally, both at home and abroad, has expressed curiosity as to the logical connection between acts such as breaking windows, firing pillar boxes, et cetera, and the vote. Only a complete lack of historical knowledge excuses that curiosity. For every advance of men's political freedom has been marked with violence and the destruction of property. Usually the advance has been marked by war, which is called glorious. Sometimes it has been marked by riotings, which are deemed less glorious but are at least effective.

We had planned a demonstration for March 4th, and this one we announced. We planned another demonstration for March 1st, but this one we did not announce. Late in the afternoon of Friday, March 1st, I drove in a taxicab, accompanied by the Hon. Secretary of the Union, Mrs Tuke and another of our members, to No. 10 Downing Street, the official residence of the Prime Minister. It was exactly half past five when we alighted from the cab and threw our stones, four of them, through the window panes. As we expected we were promptly arrested and taken to Cannon Row police station. The hour that followed will long be remembered in London. At intervals of fifteen minutes relays of women who had volunteered for the demonstration did their work. The first smashing of glass occurred in the Haymarket and

Piccadilly, and greatly startled and alarmed both pedestrians and police. A large number of the women were arrested, and everybody thought that this ended the affair. But before the excited populace and the frustrated shop owners' first exclamation had died down, before the police had reached the station with their prisoners, the ominous crashing and splintering of plate glass began again, this time along both sides of Regent Street and the Strand. A furious rush of police and people towards the second scene of action ensued. While their attention was being taken up with occurrences in this quarter, the third relay of women began breaking the windows in Oxford Circus and Bond Street. The demonstration ended for the day at half past six with the breaking of many windows in the Strand.

At the hour when this demonstration was being made a conference was being held at Scotland Yard to determine what should be done to prevent the smashing of windows on the coming Monday night. But we had not announced the hour of our March 4th protest. I had in my speech simply invited women to assemble in Parliament Square on the evening of March 4th, and they accepted the invitation.

The demonstration had taken place in the morning, when a hundred or more women walked quietly into Knightsbridge and walking singly along the streets demolished nearly every pane of glass they passed. Taken by surprise the police arrested as many as they could reach, but most of the women escaped.

For that two days' work something like two hundred Suffragettes were taken to the various police stations, and for days the long procession of women streamed through the courts. The dismayed magistrates found themselves facing, not only former rebels, but many new ones, in some cases, women whose names, like that of Dr Ethel Smyth, the composer, were famous throughout Europe. These women, when arraigned, made clear and lucid statements of their positions and their motives, but magistrates are not schooled to examine motives. They are trained to think only of laws and mostly of laws protecting property.

I was sentenced to two months' imprisonment. Others received sentences ranging from one week to two months, while those who were accused of breaking glass above five pounds in value, were committed for trial in higher courts. They were sent to prison on remand, and when the last of us were behind the grim gates, not only Holloway but three other women's prisons were taxed to provide for so many extra inmates.

I found myself in the anomalous position of a convicted offender serving two months' prison sentence, and of a prisoner on remand waiting to be charged with a more serious offence.

The trial at Old Bailey is a thing that I shall never forget. The scene is clear before me as I write, the judge impressively bewigged and scarlet robed, dominating the crowded courtroom, the solicitors at their table, the jury, and looking very far away, the anxious pale faces of our friends who crowded the narrow galleries.

The first words the Attorney General, Sir Rufus Isaacs spoke were so astoundingly unfair that I could hardly believe that I heard them aright. He began his address to the jury by telling them that they must not, on any account, connect the act of the defendants with any political agitation.

'I am very anxious to impress upon you,' he said, 'from the moment we begin to deal with the facts of this case, that all questions of whether a woman is entitled to the Parliamentary franchise, whether she should have the same right of franchise as a man, are questions which are in no sense involved in the trial of this issue. . . . Therefore, I ask you to discard altogether from the consideration of the matters which will be placed before you any viewpoint you may have on this no doubt very important political issue.'

Nevertheless Sir Rufus added in the course of his remarks that he feared that it would not be possible to keep out of the conduct of the case various references to political events, and of course the entire trial, from beginning to end, showed clearly that the case was what Mr Tim Healey, Mrs Pethick Lawrence's counsel, called it, a great State Trial.

When it came my turn to speak, realising that the average man is profoundly ignorant of the history of the women's movement—because the press has never adequately or truthfully chronicled the movement—I told the jury, as briefly as I could, the story of the forty years' peaceful agitation before my daughters and I resolved that we would give our lives to the work of getting the vote for women, and that we should use whatever means of getting the vote that were necessary to success.

'We founded the Women's Social and Political Union,' I said, 'in 1903. Our first intention was to try and influence the particular political party, which was then coming into power, to make this question of the enfranchisement of women their own question and to push it. It took some little time to convince us—and I need not weary you with the history of all that has happened—but it took some little time to convince us that that was no use; that we could not secure things in that way. Then in 1905 we faced the hard facts. We realised that there was a press boycott against Women's Suffrage. Our speeches at public meetings were not reported, our letters to the editors were not published, even if we implored the editors; even the things relating to Women's Suffrage in Parliament were not recorded. They said the subject was not of sufficient public interest to be reported in the press, and they were not prepared to report it. Then with regard to the men politicians in 1905:

we realised how shadowy were the fine phrases about democracy, about human equality, used by the gentlemen who were then coming into power. They meant to ignore the women—there was no doubt whatever about that. For in the official documents coming from the Liberal Party on the eve of the 1905 election, there were sentences like this: "What the country wants is a simple measure of Manhood Suffrage." There was no room for the inclusion of women. We knew perfectly well that if there was to be franchise reform at all, the Liberal Party which was then coming into power did not mean Votes for Women, in spite of all the pledges of members; in spite of the fact that a majority of the House of Commons, especially on the Liberal side, were pledged to it—it did not mean that they were going to put it into practice. And so we found some way of forcing their attention to this question.

'Now I come to the facts with regard to militancy. We realised that the plans we had in our minds would involve great sacrifice on our part, that it might cost us all we had. We were at that time a little organisation, composed in the main of working women, the wives and daughters of working men. And my daughters and I took a leading part, naturally, because we thought the thing out, and, to a certain extent, because we were of better social position than most of our members, and we felt a sense of responsibility.'

I described the events that marked the first days of our work, the scene in Free Trade Hall, Manchester, when my daughter and her companion were arrested for the crime of asking a question of a politician, and I continued:

'What did they do next? (I want you to realise that no step we have taken forward has been taken until after some act of repression on the part of our enemy, the Government—because it is the Government that is our enemy; it is not the members of Parliament, it is not the men in the country; it is the Government in power alone that can give us the vote. It is the Government alone that we regard as our enemy, and the whole of our agitation is directed to bringing just as much pressure as necessary upon those people who can deal with our grievance.) The next step the women took was to ask questions during the course of meetings, because, as I told you, these gentlemen gave them no opportunity of asking them afterwards. And then began the interjections of which we have heard, the interference with the right to hold public meetings, the interference with the right of free speech, of which we have heard, for which these women, these hooligan women, as they have been called—have been denounced. I ask you, gentlemen, to imagine the amount of courage which it needs for a woman to undertake that kind of work. When men come to interrupt women's meetings, they come in gangs, with noisy instruments, and sing and shout together, and stamp their feet. But when women have gone to Cabinet Ministers' meetings—only to interrupt Cabinet Ministers and nobody else—they have gone singly. And it has become increasingly difficult for them to get in, because as a result of the women's methods there has developed the system of admission by ticket and the exclusion of women—a thing which in my Liberal days would have been thought a very disgraceful thing at Liberal meetings. But this ticket system developed, and so the women could only get in with very great difficulty. Women have concealed themselves for thirty-six hours in dangerous positions, under the platforms, in the organs, wherever they could get a vantage point. They waited starving in the cold, sometimes on the roof exposed to a winter's night, just to get a chance of saying in the course of a Cabinet Minister's speech, "When is the Liberal Government going to put its promises into practice?" That has been the form militancy took in its further development.'

I went over the whole matter of our peaceful deputations, and of the violence with which they were invariably met; of our arrests and the farcical police court trials, where the mere evidence of policemen's unsupported statements sent us to prison for long terms; of the falsehoods told of us in the House of Commons by responsible members of the Government—tales of women scratching and biting policemen and using hatpins—and I accused the Government of making these attacks against women who were powerless to defend themselves because they feared the women and desired to crush the agitation represented by our organisation.

'Now it has been stated in this court,' I said, 'that it is not the Women's Social and Political Union that is in the court, but that it is certain defendants. The action of the Government, gentlemen, is certainly against the defendants who are before you here today, but it is also against the Women's Social and Political Union. The intention is to crush that organisation. And this intention apparently was arrived at after I had been sent to prison for two months for breaking a pane of glass worth, I am told, 2s. 3d., the punishment which I accepted because I was a leader of this movement, though it was an extraordinary punishment to inflict for so small an act of damages as I had committed. I accepted it as the punishment for a leader of an agitation disagreeable to the Government; and while I was there this prosecution started. They thought they would make a clean sweep of the people who they considered were the political brains of the movement. We have got many false friends in the Cabinet—people who by their words appear to be well-meaning towards the cause of Women's Suffrage. And they thought that if they could get the leaders of the Union out of the way, it would result in the indefinite postponement and settlement of the question in this country. Well, they have not succeeded in their design, and even if they had got all the so-called leaders of this movement out of their way they would not have succeeded even then. Now why have they not put the Union in the dock? We have a democratic Government, so-called. This Women's Social and Political Union is not a collection of hysterical and unimportant wild women, as has been suggested to you, but it is an important organisation, which numbers amongst its membership very important people. It is composed of women of all classes of the community, women who have influence in their particular organisations as working women; women who have influence in professional organisations as professional women; women of social importance; women even of Royal rank are amongst the members of this organisation, and so it would not pay a democratic Government to deal with this organisation as a whole.

'They hoped that by taking away the people that they thought guided the political fortunes of the organisation they would break the organisation down. They thought that if they put out of the way the influential members of the organisation they, as one member of the Cabinet, I believe, said, would crush the movement and get it "on the run." Well, Governments have many times been mistaken, gentlemen, and I venture to suggest to you that Governments are mistaken again. I think the answer to the Government was given at the Albert Hall meeting held immediately after our arrest. Within a few minutes, without the eloquence of Mrs

Pethick Lawrence, without the appeals of the people who have been called the leaders of this movement, in a very few minutes £10,000 was subscribed for the carrying on of this movement.

'Now a movement like that, supported like that, is not a wild, hysterical movement. It is not a movement of misguided people. It is a very serious movement. Women, I submit, like our members, and women, I venture to say, like the two women, and like the man who are in the dock today, are not people to undertake a thing like this lightly. May I just try to make you feel what it is that has made this movement the gigantic size it is from the very small beginnings it had? It is one of the biggest movements of modern times. A movement which is not only an influence, perhaps not yet recognised, in this country, but is influencing the women's movement all over the world. Is there anything more marvellous in modern times than the kind of spontaneous outburst in every country of this woman's movement? Even in China—and I think it somewhat of a disgrace to Englishmen— even in China women have won the vote, as an outcome of a successful revolution, with which, I dare say, members of his Majesty's Government sympathise—a bloody revolution.

'One more word on that point. When I was in prison the second time, for three months as a common criminal for no greater offence than the issue of a handbill—less inflammatory in its terms than some of the speeches of members of the Government who prosecute us here—during that time, through the efforts of a member of Parliament, there was secured for me permission to have the daily paper in prison, and the first thing I read in the daily press was this: that the Government was at that moment fêting the members of the Young Turkish Revolutionary Party, gentlemen who had invaded the privacy of the Sultan's home—we used to hear a great deal about invading the privacy of Mr Asquith's residence when we ventured to ring his door bell—gentlemen who had killed and slain, and had been successful in their revolution, while we women had never thrown a stone—for none of us was imprisoned for stone throwing, but merely for taking the part we had then taken in this organisation. There we were imprisoned while these political murderers were being fêted by the very Government who imprisoned us, and were being congratulated on the success of their revolution. Now I ask you, was it to be wondered at that women said to themselves: "Perhaps it is that we have not done enough. Perhaps it is that these gentlemen do not understand womenfolk. Perhaps they do not realise women's ways, and because we have not done the things that men have done, they may think we are not in earnest."

'And then we come down to this last business of all, when we have responsible statesmen like Mr Hobhouse saying that there had never been any sentimental uprising, no expression of feeling like that which led to the burning down of Nottingham Castle. Can you wonder, then, that we decided we should have to nerve ourselves to do more, and can you understand why we cast about to find a way, as women will, that would not involve loss of human life and the maiming of human beings, because women care more about human life than men, and I think it is quite natural that we should, for we know what life costs. We risk our lives when men are born. Now, I want to say this deliberately as a leader of this movement. We have tried to hold it back, we have tried to keep it from going beyond bounds, and I have never felt a prouder woman than I did one night when a police constable said to me, after one of these demonstrations, "Had this been a man's demonstration, there would have been bloodshed long ago." Well, my lord, there has not been any bloodshed except on the part of the women themselves—these so-called militant women. Violence has been done to us, and I who stand before you in this dock have lost a dear sister in the course of this agitation. She died within three days of coming out of prison, a little more than a year ago. These are things which, wherever we are, we do not say very much about. We cannot keep cheery, we cannot keep cheerful, we cannot keep the right kind of spirit, which means success, if we dwell too much upon the hard part of our agitation. But I do say this, gentlemen, that whatever in future you may think of us, you will say this about us, that whatever our enemies may say, we have always put up an honourable fight, and taken no unfair means of defeating our opponents, although they have not always been people who have acted so honourably towards us.

'We have assaulted no one; we have done no hurt to any one; and it was not until "Black Friday"—and what happened on "Black Friday" is that we had a new Home Secretary, and there appeared to be new orders given to the police, because the police on that occasion showed a kind of ferocity in dealing with the women that they had never done before, and the women came to us and said: "We cannot bear this"—it was not until then we felt this new form of repression should compel us to take another step. That is the question of "Black Friday," and I want to say here and now that every effort was made after "Black Friday" to get an open public judicial inquiry into the doings of "Black Friday," as to the instructions given to the police. That inquiry was refused; but an informal inquiry was held by a man, whose name will carry conviction as to his status and moral integrity on the one side of the great political parties, and a man of equal standing on the Liberal side. These two men were Lord Robert Cecil and Mr Ellis Griffith. They held a private inquiry, had women before them, took their evidence, examined that evidence, and after hearing it said that they believed what the women had told them was substantially true, and that they thought there was good cause for that inquiry to be held. That was embodied in a report. To show you our difficulties, Lord Robert Cecil, in a speech at the Criterion Restaurant, spoke on this question. He called upon the Government to hold this inquiry, and not one word of that speech was reported in any morning paper. That is the sort of thing we have had to face, and I welcome standing here, if only for the purpose of getting these facts out, and I challenge the Attorney General to institute an inquiry into these proceedings—not that kind of inquiry of sending their inspectors to Holloway and accepting what they are told by the officials—but to open a public inquiry, with a jury, if he likes, to deal with our grievances against the Government and the methods of this agitation.

'I say it is not the defendants who have conspired, but the Government who have conspired against us to crush this agitation; but however the matter may be decided, we are content to abide by the verdict of posterity. We are not the kind of people who like to brag a lot; we are not the kind of people who would bring ourselves into this position unless we were convinced that it was the only way. I have tried—all my life I have worked for this question—I have tried arguments, I have tried persuasion. I have addressed a greater number of public meetings, perhaps, than any person in this court, and I have never addressed one meeting where substantially the opinion of the meeting—not a ticket meeting, but an open meeting, for I have never addressed any other kind of a meeting—has not been that where women bear burdens and share responsibilities like men they should be given the privileges that men enjoy. I am convinced that public opinion is with us—that it has been stifled—wilfully stifled—so that in a public court of justice one is glad of being allowed to speak on this question.'

The jury was absent for more than an hour, showing that they had some difficulty in agreeing upon a verdict. When they returned it was plain from their strained countenances that they were labouring under deep feeling. The foreman's voice shook as he pronounced the verdict, guilty as charged, and he had hard work to control his emotion as he added: 'Your lordship, we unanimously desire to express the hope that, taking into consideration the undoubtedly pure motives that underlie the agitation that has led to this trouble, you will be pleased to exercise the utmost clemency and leniency in dealing with the case.'

A burst of applause followed this plea. Then Mr Pethick Lawrence arose and asked to say a few words before sentence was pronounced. He said that it must be evident, aside from the jury's recommendation, that we had been actuated by political motives, and that we were in fact political offenders. It had been decided in English courts that political offenders were different from ordinary offenders, and Mr Lawrence cited the case of a Swiss subject whose extradition was refused because of the political character of his offence. The court on that occasion had declared that even if the crime were murder committed with a political motive it was a political crime. Mr Lawrence also reminded the judge of the case of the late Mr W. T. Stead, convicted of a crime, yet because of the unusual motive behind the crime, was allowed first division treatment and full freedom to receive his family and friends. Last of all the case of Dr Jameson was cited. Although his raid resulted in the death of twenty-one persons and the wounding of forty-six more, the political character of his offence was taken into account and he was made a first division prisoner.

They were men, fighting in a man's war. We of the WSPU were women, fighting in a woman's war. Lord Coleridge, therefore, saw in us only reckless and criminal defiers of law. Lord Coleridge said: 'You have been convicted of a crime for which the law would sanction, if I chose to impose it, a sentence of two years' imprisonment with hard labour. There are circumstances connected with your case which the jury have very properly brought to my attention, and I have been asked by you all three to treat you as first class misdemeanants. If, in the course of this case, I had observed any contrition or disavowal of the acts you have committed, or any hope that you would avoid repetition of them in future, I should have been very much prevailed upon by the arguments that have been advanced to me.'

No contrition having been expressed by us, the sentence of the court was that we were to suffer imprisonment, in the second division, for the term of nine months, and that we were to pay the costs of the prosecution.

All during that summer militancy surged up and down throughout the Kingdom. A series of attacks on golf links was instituted, not at all in a spirit of wanton mischief, but with the direct and very practical object of reminding the dull and self-satisfied English public that when the liberties of English women were being stolen from them was no time to think of sports. The women selected country clubs where prominent Liberal politicians were wont to take their week-end pleasures, and with acids they burned great patches of turf, rendering the golf greens useless for the time being. They burned the words, Votes for Women, in some cases, and always they left behind them reminders that women were warring for their freedom. On one occasion when the Court was at Balmoral Castle in Scotland, the Suffragettes invaded the Royal golf links, and when Sunday morning dawned all the marking flags were found to have been replaced by WSPU flags bearing inscriptions such as 'Votes for Women means peace for Ministers,' 'Forcible feeding must be stopped,' and the like. The golf links were frequently visited by Suffragettes in order to question recreant ministers. Two women followed the Prime Minister to Inverness, where he was playing golf with Mr McKenna. Approaching the men one Suffragette exclaimed: 'Mr Asquith, you must stop forcible feeding—' She got no farther, for Mr Asquith, turning pale with rage—perhaps—retreated behind the Home Secretary, who, quite forgetting his manners, seized the Suffragette, crying out that he was going to throw her into the pond. 'Then we will take you with us,' the two retorted, after which a very lively scuffle ensued, and the women were not thrown into the pond.

This golf green activity really aroused more hostility against us than all the window-breaking. The papers published appeals to us not to interfere with a game that helped weary politicians to think clearly, but our reply to this was that it had not had any such effect on the Prime Minister or Mr Lloyd-George. We had undertaken to spoil their sport and that of a large class of comfortable men in order that they should be obliged to think clearly about women, and women's firm determination to get justice.

I made my return to active work in the autumn by speaking at a great meeting of the WSPU, held in the Albert Hall.

I went on to survey the situation in which the WSPU now stood and to outline the new militant policy which we had decided upon. This policy, to begin with, was relentless opposition, not only to the party in power, the Liberal Party, but to all parties in the coalition. I reminded the women that the Government that had tricked and betrayed us and was now plotting to make our progress towards citizenship doubly difficult, was kept in office through the coalition of three parties. There was the Liberal Party, nominally the governing party, but they could not live another day without the coalition of the Nationalist and the Labour parties. So we should say, not only to the Liberal Party but to the Nationalist Party and the Labour Party, 'So long as you keep in office an anti-suffrage Government, you are parties to their guilt, and from henceforth we offer you the same opposition which we give to the people whom you are keeping in power with your support.' I said further: 'We have summoned the Labour Party to do their duty by their own programme, and to go into opposition to the Government on every question until the Government do justice to women. They apparently are not willing to do that. Some of them tell us that other things are more important than the liberty of women— than the liberty of working women. We say, "Then, gentlemen, we must teach you the value of your own principles, and until you are prepared to stand for the right of women to decide their lives and the laws under which they shall live, you, with Mr Asquith and company, are equally responsible for all that has happened and is happening to women in this struggle for emancipation.'"

Outlining further our new and stronger policy of aggression, I said: 'There is a great deal of criticism, ladies and gentlemen, of this movement. It always seems to me when the anti-suffrage members of the Government criticise militancy in women that it is very like beasts of prey reproaching the gentler animals who turn in desperate resistance when at the point of death. Criticism from gentlemen who do not hesitate to order out armies to kill and slay their opponents, who do not hesitate to encourage party mobs to attack defenceless women in public meetings—criticism from them hardly rings true. Then I get letters from people who tell me that they are ardent suffragists but who say that they do not like the recent developments in the militant movement, and implore me to urge the members not to be reckless with human life. Ladies and gentlemen, the only recklessness the militant suffragists have shown about human life has been about their own lives and not about the lives of others, and I say here and now that it has never been and never will be the policy of the Women's Social and Political Union recklessly to endanger human life. We leave that to the enemy. We leave that to the men in their warfare. It is not the method of women. No, even from the point of view of public policy, militancy affecting the security of human life would be out of place. *There is something that governments care far more for than human life, and that is the security of property, and so it is through property that we shall strike the enemy.* From henceforward the women who agree with me will say, "We disregard your laws, gentlemen, we set the liberty and the dignity and the welfare of women above all such considerations, and we shall continue this war, as we have done in the past; and what sacrifice of property, or what injury to property accrues will not be our fault. It will be the fault of that Government who admit the justice of our demands, but refuses to concede them without the evidence, so they have told us, afforded to governments of the past, that those who asked for liberty were in earnest in their demands!'"

I called upon the women of the meeting to join me in this new militancy, and I reminded them anew that the women who were fighting in the Suffragette army had a great mission, the greatest mission the world has ever known—the freeing of one-half the human race, and through that freedom the saving of the other half. I said to them: 'Be militant each in your own way. Those of you who can express your militancy by going to the House of Commons and refusing to leave without satisfaction, as we did in the early days—do so. Those of you who can express militancy by facing party mobs at Cabinet Ministers' meetings, when you remind them of their falseness to principle—do so. Those of you who can express your militancy by joining us in our anti-Government by-election policy—do so. Those of you who can break windows—break them. Those of you who can still further attack the secret idol of property, so as to make the Government realise that property is as greatly endangered by women's suffrage as it was by the Chartists of old—do so. And my last word is to the Government: I incite this meeting to rebellion. I say to the Government: You have not dared to take the leaders of Ulster for their incitement to rebellion. Take me if you dare, but if you dare I tell you this, that so long as those who incited to armed rebellion and the destruction of human life in Ulster are at liberty, you will not keep me in prison. So long as men rebels—and voters—are at liberty, we will not remain in prison, first division or no first division.'

I ask my readers, some of whom no doubt will be shocked and displeased at these words of mine that I have so frankly set down, to put themselves in the place of those women who for years had given their lives entirely and unstintingly to the work of securing political freedom for women; who had converted so great a proportion of the electorate that, had the House of Commons been a free body, we should have won that freedom years before; who had seen their freedom withheld from them through treachery and misuse of power. I ask you to consider that we had used, in our agitation, only peaceful means until we saw clearly that peaceful means were absolutely of no avail, and then for years we had used only the mildest militancy, until we were taunted by Cabinet Ministers, and told that we should never get the vote until we employed the same violence that men had used in their agitation for suffrage. After that we had used stronger militancy, but even that, by comparison with the militancy of men in labour disputes, could not possibly be counted as violent. Through all these stages of our agitation we had been punished with the greatest severity, sent to prison like common criminals, and of late years tortured as no criminals have been tortured for a century in civilised countries of the world. And during all these years we had seen disastrous strikes that had caused suffering and death, to say nothing at all of the enormous economic waste, and we had never seen a single strike leader punished as we had been. We, who had suffered sentences of nine months' imprisonment for inciting women to mild rebellion, had seen a labour leader who had done his best to incite an army to mutiny released from prison in two months by the Government. And now we had come to a point where we saw civil war threatened, where we read in the papers every day reports of speeches a thousand times more incendiary than anything we had ever said. We heard prominent members of Parliament openly declaring that if the

Home Rule Bill was passed Ulster would fight, and Ulster would be right. None of these men were arrested. Instead they were applauded. Lord Selborne, one of our sternest critics, referring to the fact that Ulstermen were drilling under arms, said publicly: 'The method which the people of Ulster are adopting to show the depths of their convictions and the intensity of their feelings will impress the imagination of the whole country.' But Lord Selborne was not arrested. Neither were the mutinous officers who resigned their commissions when ordered to report for duty against the men of Ulster who were actually preparing for civil war.

What does all this mean? Why is it that men's blood-shedding militancy is applauded and women's symbolic militancy punished with a prison cell and the forcible feeding horror? It means simply this, that men's double standard of sex morals, whereby the victims of their lust are counted as outcasts, while the men themselves escape all social censure, really applies to morals in all departments of life. Men make the moral code and they expect women to accept it. They have decided that it is entirely right and proper for men to fight for their liberties and their rights, but that it is not right and proper for women to fight for theirs.

They have decided that for men to remain silently quiescent while tyrannical rulers impose bonds of slavery upon them is cowardly and dishonourable, but that for women to do that same thing is not

cowardly and dishonourable, but merely respectable.
Well, the Suffragettes absolutely repudiate that
double standard of morals. If it is right for men to
fight for their freedom, and God knows what the
human race would be like today if men had not,
since time began, fought for their freedom, then it
is right for women to fight for their freedom and
the freedom of the children they bear. On this
declaration of faith the militant women of England
rest their case.

Now we indeed lighted the torch, and we did it
with the absolute conviction that no other course
was open to us. We had tried every other measure,
as I am sure that I have demonstrated to my readers,
and our years of work and suffering and sacrifice
had taught us that the Government would not yield
to right and justice, what the majority of members
of the House of Commons admitted was right and
justice, but that the Government would, as other
governments invariably do, yield to expediency.
Now our task was to show the Government that
it was expedient to yield to the women's just
demands. In order to do that we had to make
England and every department of English life
insecure and unsafe. We had to make English law
a failure and the courts farce comedy theatres; we
had to discredit the Government and Parliament
in the eyes of the world; we had to spoil English
sports, hurt business, destroy valuable property,

demoralise the world of society, shame the churches, upset the whole orderly conduct of life—

That is, we had to do as much of this guerilla warfare as the people of England would tolerate. When they came to the point of saying to the Government: 'Stop this, in the only way it can be stopped, by giving the women of England representation,' then we should extinguish our torch.

In the first month of guerilla warfare an enormous amount of property was damaged and destroyed. On January 31st a number of putting greens were burned with acids; on February 7th and 8th telegraph and telephone wires were cut in several places and for some hours all communication between London and Glasgow were suspended; a few days later windows in various of London's smartest clubs were broken, and the orchid houses at Kew were wrecked and many valuable blooms destroyed by cold. The jewel room at the Tower of London was invaded and a showcase broken. The residence of H. R. H. Prince Christian and Lambeth Palace, seat of the Archbishop of Canterbury, were visited and had windows broken. The refreshment house in Regents Park was burned to the ground on February 12th and on February 18th a country house which was being built at Walton-on-the-Hill for Mr Lloyd-George was partially destroyed, a bomb having been exploded in the early morning before the arrival of the workmen. A hatpin and a hairpin picked up near the house—coupled with the fact that care had been taken not to endanger any lives—led the police to believe that the deed had been done by women enemies of Mr Lloyd-George. Four days later I was arrested and brought up in Epsom police court, where I was charged with having 'counselled and procured' the persons who did the damage. Admitted to bail for the night, I appeared next morning in court, where the case was fully reviewed. Speeches of mine were read, one speech, made at a meeting held on January 22nd, in which I called for volunteers to act with me in a particular engagement; and another, made the day after the explosion, in which I publicly accepted responsibility for all militant acts done in the past, and even for what had been done at Walton. At the conclusion of the hearing I was committed for trial at the May Assizes at Guildford. Bail would be allowed, it was stated, if I would agree to give the usual undertaking to refrain from all militancy or incitement to militancy.

I asked that the case be set for speedy trial at the Assizes then in progress. I was entirely willing, I said, to give an undertaking for a short period, for a week, or even two weeks, but I could not possibly do so for a much longer period, looking at the fact that a new session of Parliament began in March, and was vitally concerned with the interests of women. The request was refused, and I was ordered to be taken to Holloway. I warned the magistrate that I should at once adopt the hunger strike, and I told him that if I lived at all until the summer it would be a dying woman who would come up for trial.

Arriving at Holloway I carried out my intention, but within twenty-four hours I heard that the authorities had arranged that my trial should take place on April 1st, instead of at the end of June, and at the Central Criminal Court, London, instead of the Guildford Court. I then gave the required undertakings and was immediately released on bail.

When I entered Old Bailey on that memorable Wednesday, April 2nd, 1913, to be tried for inciting to commit a felony, the court was packed with women. A great crowd of women who could not obtain the necessary tickets remained in the streets below for hours waiting news of the trial. A large number of detectives from Scotland Yard, and a still larger number of uniformed police were on duty both inside and outside the court. I could not imagine why it was considered necessary to have such a regiment of police on hand, for I had not, at that time, realised the state of terror into which the militant movement, in its new development, had thrown the authorities.

Mr Bodkin and Mr Travers Humphreys appeared to prosecute on behalf of the Crown, and I conducted my own case, in consultation with my solicitor, Mr Marshall. The Judge, Mr Justice Lush, having taken his seat I entered the dock and listened to the reading of the indictment. I pled 'not guilty,' not because I wished to evade responsibility for the explosion,—I had already assumed that responsibility—but because the indictment accused me of having wickedly and maliciously incited women to crime. What I had done was not wicked of purpose, but quite the opposite of wicked. I could not therefore truthfully plead guilty.

Mr Bodkin opened the case by explaining the 'Malicious Damages to Property Act' of 1861, under which I was charged, and after describing the explosion which had damaged the Lloyd-George house at Walton, said that I was accused of being in the affair an accessory before the fact. It was not suggested, he said, that I was present when the crime was committed, but it was charged that I had moved and incited, counselled and procured women whose names were unknown to carry out that crime. It would be for the jury to decide, after the evidence had been presented, whether the facts did not point most clearly to the conclusion that women, probably two in number, who committed the crime were members of the Women's Social and Political Union, which had its office in Kingsway in London, and of which the defendant was the head, moving spirit and recognised leader.

Many extracts from my speeches made in January and February were read, and the final speech made just before my arrest at Chelsea.

Witnesses were then examined; the carter who heard and reported the explosion; the foreman in charge of the damaged house, who told the cost of the damages, and described the explosives, etc., found on the premises; several police officers who told of finding hairpins and a woman's rubber golosh in the house, and so on. Absolutely nothing was brought out that tended to show that the Suffragettes had anything to do with the affair.

Proceedings were resumed on the following day, and the examination of witnesses for the prosecution went on. At the close of the examination, the Judge inquired whether I desired to call any witnesses. I replied:

'I do not desire to give evidence or to call any witnesses, but I desire to address your lordship.'

I began by objecting to some of the things Mr Bodkin had said in his speech which concerned me personally. He had referred to me—or at least his words conveyed the suggestion—that I was a woman riding about in my motor car inciting other women to do acts which entail imprisonment and great suffering, while I, perhaps indulging in some curious form of pleasure, was protected, or thought myself protected, from serious consequences. I said that Mr Bodkin knew perfectly well that I shared all the dangers the other women faced, that I had been in prison three times, serving two of the sentences in full, and being treated like an ordinary felon—searched, put in prison clothes, eating prison fare, given solitary confinement and conforming to all the abominable rules imposed upon women who commit crimes in England. I thought I owed it to myself, especially as the same suggestions—in regard to the luxury in which I lived, supported by the members of the WSPU—had been made, not only by Mr Bodkin in court, but by members of the Government in the House of Commons—I thought I owed it to myself to say that I owned no motor car and never had owned one. The car in which I occasionally rode was owned by the organisation and was used for general propaganda work. In that car, and in cars owned by friends I had gone about my work as a speaker in the Woman Suffrage movement. It was equally untrue, I said, that some of us were making incomes of £1,000 to £1,500 a year out of the suffrage movement, as had actually been alleged in the debates in the House in which members of Parliament were trying to decide how to crush militancy. No woman in our organisation was making any such income, or anything remotely like it. Myself, I had sacrificed a considerable portion of my income because I had to surrender a very important part of it in order to be free to do what I thought was my duty in the movement.

Addressing myself to my defence I told the court that it was a very serious condition of things when a large number of respectable and naturally law abiding people, people of upright lives, came to hold the law in contempt, came seriously to making up their minds that they were justified in breaking the law. 'The whole of good government,' I said, 'rests upon acceptance of the law, upon respect of the law, and I say to you seriously, my lord, and gentlemen of the jury, that women of intelligence, women of training, women of upright life, have for many years ceased to respect the laws of this country. It is an absolute fact, and when you look at the laws of this country as they affect women it is not to be wondered at.'

At some length I went over these laws, laws that made it possible for the Judge to send me, if found guilty, to prison for fourteen years, while the maximum penalty for offences of the most revolting kind against little girls was only two years' imprisonment. The laws of inheritance, the laws of divorce, the laws of guardianship of children—all so scandalously unjust to women, I sketched briefly, and I said that not only these laws and others, but the administration of the laws fell so far short of adequacy that women felt that they must be permitted to share the work of cleaning up the entire situation. I tried here to tell of certain dreadful things that I had learned as the wife of a barrister, things about some of the men in high places who are entrusted with the administration of the law, of a judge of Assizes where many hideous crimes against women were tried, this judge himself being found dead one morning in a brothel, but the court would not allow me to go into personalities, as he called it, with regard to 'distinguished people,' and told me that the sole question before the jury was whether or not I was guilty as charged. I must speak on that subject and on no other.

After a hard fight to be allowed to tell the jury the reasons why women had lost respect for the law, and were making such a struggle in order to become law makers themselves, I closed my speech by saying:

'Over one thousand women have gone to prison in the course of this agitation, have suffered their imprisonment, have come out of prison injured in health, weakened in body, but not in spirit. I come to stand my trial from the bedside of one of my daughters, who has come out of Holloway Prison, sent there for two months' hard labour for participating with four other people in breaking a small pane of glass. She has hunger-struck in prison. She submitted herself for more than five weeks to the horrible ordeal of feeding by force, and she has come out of prison having lost nearly two stone in weight. She is so weak that she cannot get out of her bed. And I say to you, gentlemen, that is the kind of punishment you are inflicting upon me or any other woman who may be brought before you. I ask you if you are prepared to send an incalculable number of women to prison—I speak to you as representing others in the same position—if you are prepared to go on doing that kind of thing indefinitely, because that is what is going to happen. There is absolutely no doubt about it. I think you have seen enough even in this present case to convince you that we are not women who are notoriety hunters. We could get that, heaven knows, much more cheaply if we sought it. We are women, rightly or wrongly, convinced that this is the only way in which we can win power to alter what for us are intolerable conditions, absolutely intolerable conditions. A London clergyman only the other day said that sixty per cent of the married women in his parish were breadwinners, supporting their husbands as well as their children. When you think of the wages women earn, when you think of what this means to the future of the children of this country, I ask you to take this question very, very seriously. Only this morning I have had information brought to me which could be supported by sworn affidavits, that there is in this country, in this very city of London of ours, a regulated traffic, not only in women of full age, but in little children; that they are being purchased, that they are being entrapped, and that they are being trained to minister to the vicious pleasures of persons who ought to know better in their positions of life.

'Well, these are the things that have made us women determined to go on, determined to face everything, determined to see this thing out to the end, let it cost us what it may. And if you convict me, gentlemen, if you find me guilty, I tell you quite honestly and quite frankly, that whether the sentence is a long sentence, whether the sentence is a short sentence, I shall not submit to it. I shall, the moment I leave this court, if I am sent to prison, whether to penal servitude or to the lighter form of imprisonment—because I am not sufficiently versed in the law to know what his lordship may decide; but whatever my sentence is, from the moment I leave this court I shall quite deliberately refuse to eat food—I shall join the women who are already in Holloway on the hunger strike. I shall come out of prison, dead or alive, at the earliest possible moment; and once out again, as soon as I am physically fit I shall enter into this fight again. Life is very dear to all of us. I am not seeking, as was said by the Home Secretary, to commit suicide. I do not want to commit suicide. I want to see the women of this country enfranchised, and I want to live until that is done. Those are the feelings by which we are animated. We offer ourselves as sacrifices, just as your forefathers did in the past, in this cause, and I would ask you all to put this question to yourselves:—Have you the right, as human beings, to condemn another human being to death— because that is what it amounts to? Can you throw the first stone? Have you the right to judge women?

'You have not the right in human justice, not the right by the constitution of this country, if rightly interpreted, to judge me, because you are not my peers. You know, every one of you, that I should not be standing here, that I should not break one single law—if I had the rights that you possess, if I had a share in electing those who make the laws I have to obey; if I had a voice in controlling the taxes I am called upon to pay, I should not be standing here. And I say to you it is a very serious state of things. I say to you, my lord, it is a very serious situation, that women of upright life, women who have devoted the best of their years to the public weal, that women who are engaged in trying to undo some of the terrible mistakes that men in their government of the country have made, because after all, in the last resort, men are responsible for the present state of affairs—I put it to you that it is a very serious situation. You are not accustomed to deal with people like me in the ordinary discharge of your duties; but you are called upon to deal with people who break the law from selfish motives. I break the law from no selfish motive. I have no personal end to serve, neither have any of the other women who have gone through this court during the past few weeks, like sheep to the slaughter. Not one of these women would, if women were free, be law-breakers. They are women who seriously believe that this hard path that they are treading is the only path to their enfranchisement. They seriously believe that the welfare of humanity demands this sacrifice; they believe that the horrible evils which are ravaging our civilisation will never be removed until women get the vote. They know that the very fount of life is being poisoned; they know that homes are being destroyed; that because of bad education, because of the unequal standard of morals, even the mothers and children are destroyed by one of the vilest and most horrible diseases that ravage humanity.

'There is only one way to put a stop to this agitation; there is only one way to break down this agitation. It is not by deporting us, it is not by locking us up in gaol; it is by doing us justice. And so I appeal to you gentlemen, in this case of mine, to give a verdict, not only on my case, but upon the whole of this agitation. I ask you to find me not guilty of malicious incitement to a breach of the law.

'These are my last words. My incitement is not malicious. If I had power to deal with these things, I would be in absolute obedience to the law. I would say to women, "You have a constitutional means of getting redress for your grievances; use your votes, convince your fellow-voters of the righteousness of your demands. That is the way to obtain justice." I am not guilty of malicious incitement, and I appeal to you, for the welfare of the country, for the welfare of the race, to return a verdict of not guilty in this case that you are called upon to try.'

After recapitulating the charge the Judge, in summing up, said:

'It is scarcely necessary for me to tell you that the topics urged by the defendant in her address to you with regard to provocation by the laws of the country and the injustice done to women because they are not given the vote as men are, have no bearing upon the question you have to decide.

'The motive at the back of her mind, or at the back of the minds of those who actually did put the gunpowder there, would afford no defence to this indictment. I am quite sure you will deal with this case upon the evidence, and the evidence alone, without regard to any question as to whether you think the law is just or unjust. It has nothing to do with the case. I should think you will probably have no doubt that this defendant, if she did these things charged against her, is not actuated by the ordinary selfish motive that leads most of the criminals who are in this dock to commit the crimes that they do commit. She is none the less guilty if she did these things which are charged against her, although she believes that by means of this kind the condition of society will be altered.'

The jury retired, and soon after the afternoon session of the court opened they filed in, and in reply to the usual question asked by the clerk of arraigns, said that they had agreed upon a verdict. Said the clerk:

'Do you find Mrs Pankhurst guilty or not guilty?'

'Guilty,' said the foreman, 'with a strong recommendation to mercy.'

I spoke once more to the Judge.

'The jury have found me guilty, with a strong recommendation to mercy, and I do not see, since motive is not taken into account in human laws, that they could do otherwise after your summing up. But since motive is not taken into account in human laws, and since I, whose motives are not ordinary motives, am about to be sentenced by you to the punishment which is accorded to people whose motives are selfish motives, I have only this to say: If it was impossible for a different verdict to be found; if it is your duty to sentence me, as it will be presently, then I want to say to you, as a private citizen, and to the jury as private citizens, that I, standing here, found guilty by the laws of my country, I say to you it is your duty, as private citizens, to do what you can to put an end to this intolerable state of affairs. I put that duty upon you. And I want to say, *whatever the sentence you pass upon me, I shall do what is humanly possible to terminate that sentence at the earliest possible moment. I have no sense of guilt. I feel I have done my duty. I look upon myself as a prisoner of war. I am under no moral obligation to conform to, or in any way accept, the sentence imposed upon me.* I shall take the desperate remedy that other women have taken. It is obvious to you that the struggle will be an unequal one, but I shall make it—I shall make it as long as I have an ounce of strength left in me, or any life left in me.

'I shall fight, I shall fight, I shall fight, from the moment I enter prison to struggle against overwhelming odds; I shall resist the doctors if they attempt to feed me. I was sentenced last May in this court to nine months' imprisonment. I remained in prison six weeks. There are people who have laughed at the ordeal of hunger-striking and forcible feeding. All I can say is, and the doctors can bear me out, that I was released because, had I remained there much longer, I should have been a dead woman.

'I know what it is because I have gone through it. My own daughter[1] has only just left it. There are women there still facing that ordeal, facing it twice a day. Think of it, my lord, twice a day this fight is gone through. Twice a day a weak woman resisting overwhelming force, fights and fights as long as she has strength left; fights against women and even against men, resisting with her tongue, with her teeth, this ordeal. Last night in the House of Commons some alternative was discussed, or rather, some additional punishment. Is it not a strange thing, my lord, that laws which have sufficed to restrain men throughout the history of this country do not suffice now to restrain women— decent women, honourable women?

---

[1] Sylvia Pankhurst, who was forcibly fed for five weeks, during an original sentence of two months imposed for breaking one window.

'Well, my lord, I do want you to realise it. I am not whining about my punishment. I invited it. I deliberately broke the law, not hysterically or emotionally, but of set serious purpose, because I honestly feel it is the only way. Now, I put the responsibility of what is to follow upon you, my lord, as a private citizen, and upon the gentlemen of the jury, as private citizens, and upon all the men in this court—what are you, with your political powers, going to do to end this intolerable situation?

'*To the women I have represented, to the women who, in response to my incitement, have faced these terrible consequences, have broken laws, to them I want to say I am not going to fail them, but to face it as they face it, to go through with it, and I know that they will go on with the fight whether I live or whether I die.*

'*This movement will go on and on until we have the rights of citizens in this country, as women have in our Colonies, as they will have throughout the civilised world before this woman's war is ended.*

'That is all I have to say.'

Mr Justice Lush, in passing sentence, said: 'It is my duty, Mrs Emmeline Pankhurst, and a very painful duty it is, to pass what, in my opinion, is a suitable and adequate sentence for the crime of which you have been most properly convicted, having regard to the strong recommendation to mercy by the jury. I quite recognise, as I have already said, that the motives that have actuated you in committing this crime are not the selfish motives that actuate most of the persons who stand in your position, but although you blind your eyes to it, I cannot help pointing out to you that the crime of which you have been convicted is not only a very serious one, but, in spite of your motives, it is, in fact, a wicked one. It is wicked because it not only leads to the destruction of property of persons who have done you no wrong, but in spite of your calculations, it may expose other people to the danger of being maimed or even killed. It is wicked because you are, and have been, luring other people —young women, it may be—to engage in such crimes, possibly to their own ruin; and it is wicked, because you cannot help being alive to it if you would only think.

'You are setting an example to other persons who may have other grievances that they legitimately want to have put right by embarking on a similar scheme to yours, and trying to effect their object by attacking the property, if not the lives, of other people. I know, unfortunately—at least, I feel sure— you will pay no heed to what I say. I only beg of you to think of these things.'

'I have thought of them,' I interjected.

'Think, if only for one short hour, dispassionately,' continued the majesty of law, 'I can only say that, although the sentence I am going to pass must be a severe one, must be adequate to the crime of which you have been found guilty, if you would only realise the wrong you are doing, and the mistake you are making, and would see the error you have committed, and undertake to amend matters by using your influence in a right direction, I would be the first to use all my best endeavours to bring about a mitigation of the sentence I am about to pass.

'I cannot, and I will not, regard your crime as a merely trivial one. It is not. It is a most serious one, and, whatever you may think, it is a wicked one. I have paid regard to the recommendation of the jury. You yourself have stated the maximum sentence which this particular offence is by the legislature thought to deserve. The least sentence I can pass upon you is a sentence of three years' penal servitude.'

As soon as the sentence was pronounced the intense silence which had reigned throughout the trial was broken, and an absolute pandemonium broke out among the spectators. At first it was merely a confused and angry murmur of 'Shame!' 'Shame!' The murmurs quickly swelled into loud and indignant cries, and then from gallery and court there arose a great chorus uttered with the utmost intensity and passion. 'Shame!' 'Shame!' The women sprang to their feet, in many instances stood on their seats, shouting 'Shame!' 'Shame!' as I was conducted out of the dock in charge of two wardresses. 'Keep the flag flying!' shouted a woman's voice, and the response came in a chorus: 'We will!'

'Bravo!' 'Three cheers for Mrs Pankhurst!' That was the last I heard of the courtroom protest.

Afterwards I heard that the noise and confusion was kept up for several minutes longer, the Judge and the police being quite powerless to obtain order. Then the women filed out singing the Women's Marsellaise—

> 'March on, march on,
> Face to the dawn,
> The dawn of liberty.'

The Judge flung after their retreating forms the dire threat of prison for any woman who dared repeat such a scene. Threat of prison—to Suffragettes! The women's song only swelled the louder and the corridors of Old Bailey reverberated with their shouts. Certainly that venerable building had never in its checkered history witnessed such a scene. The great crowd of detectives and police who were on duty seemed actually paralysed by the audacity of the protest, for they made no attempt to intervene.

At three o'clock, when I left the court by a side entrance in Newgate Street, I found a crowd of women waiting to cheer me. With the two wardresses I entered a four wheeler and was driven to Holloway to begin my hunger strike. Scores of women followed in taxicabs, and when I arrived at the prison gates there was another protest of cheers for the cause and boos for the law. In the midst of all this intense excitement I passed through the grim gates into the twilight of prison, now become a battleground.

Every step since that meeting in October, 1912, when we definitely declared war on the peace of England, has been beset with danger and difficulty, often unexpected and undeclared. In October, 1913, I sailed in the French liner, *La Provence*, for my third visit to the United States. My intention was published in the public press of England, France and America. No attempt at concealment of my purpose was made, and in fact, my departure was witnessed by two men from Scotland Yard. Some hints had reached my ears that an attempt would be made by the Immigration Officers at the port of New York to exclude me as an undesirable alien, but I gave little credit to these reports. American friends wrote and cabled encouraging words, and so I passed my time aboard ship quite peacefully, working part of the time, resting also against the fatigue always attendant on a lecture tour.

We came to anchor in the harbour of New York on October 26th, and there, to my astonishment, the Immigration authorities notified me that I was ordered to Ellis Island to appear before a Board of Special Inquiry. The officers who served the order of detention did so with all courtesy, even with a certain air of reluctance. They allowed my American travelling companion, Mrs Rheta Childe Dorr, to accompany me to the Island, but no one, not even the solicitor sent by Mrs O. H. P. Belmont to defend me, was permitted to attend me before the Board of Special Inquiry. I went before these three men quite alone, as many a poor, friendless woman, without any of my resources, has had to appear. The moment of my entrance to the room I knew that extraordinary means had been employed against me, for on the desk behind which the Board sat I saw a complete *dossier* of my case in English legal papers. These papers may have been supplied by Scotland Yard, or they may have been supplied by the Government. I cannot tell, of course. They sufficed to convince the Board of Special Inquiry that I was a person of doubtful character, to say the least of it, and I was informed that I should have to be detained until the higher authorities at Washington examined my case. Everything was done to make me comfortable, the rooms of the Commissioner of Immigration being turned over to me and my companion. The very men who found me guilty of moral obloquy—something of which no British jury has ever yet accused me—put themselves out in a number of ways to make my detention agreeable. I was escorted all over the Island and through the quarters assigned detained immigrants, whose right to land in the United States is in question. The huge dining-rooms, the spotless kitchens and the admirably varied bill of fare interested and impressed me. Nothing like them exists in any English institution.

I remained at Ellis Island two and a half days, long enough for the Commissioner of Immigration at Washington to take my case to the President who instantly ordered my release. Whoever was responsible for my detention entirely overlooked the advertising value of the incident. My lecture tour was made much more successful for it and I embarked for England late in November with a very generous American contribution to our war chest, a contribution, alas, that I was not permitted to deliver in person.

The night before the White Star liner *Majestic* reached Plymouth a wireless message from headquarters informed me that the Government had decided to arrest me on my arrival. The arrest was made, under very dramatic conditions, the next day shortly before noon. The steamer came to anchor in the outer harbour, and we saw at once that the bay, usually so animated with passing vessels, had been cleared of all craft. Far in the distance the tender, which on other occasions had always met the steamer, rested at anchor between two huge grey warships. For a moment or two the scene halted, the passengers crowding to the deckrails in speechless curiosity to see what was to happen next. Suddenly a fisherman's dory, power driven, dashed across the harbour, directly under the noses of the grim war vessels. Two women, spray drenched, stood up in the boat, and as it ploughed swiftly past our steamer the women called out to me: 'The Cats are here, Mrs Pankhurst! They're close on you—' Their voices trailed away into the mist and we heard no more. Within a minute or two a frightened ship's boy appeared on deck and delivered a message from the purser asking me to step down to his office. I answered that I would certainly do nothing of the kind, and next the police swarmed out on deck and I heard, for the fifth time that I was arrested under the Cat and Mouse Act. They had sent five men from Scotland Yard, two men from Plymouth and a wardress from Holloway, a sufficient number, it will be allowed, to take one woman from a ship anchored two miles out at sea.

Following my firm resolve not to assist in any way the enforcing of the infamous law I refused to go with the men, who thereupon picked me up and carried me to the waiting police tender. We steamed some miles up the Cornish coast, the police refusing absolutely to tell me whither they were conveying me, and finally disembarked at Bull Point, a Government landing-stage, closed to the general public. Here a motor car was waiting, and accompanied by my bodyguard from Scotland Yard and Holloway, I was driven across Dartmoor to Exeter, where I had a not unendurable imprisonment and hunger strike of four days. Everyone from the Governor of the prison to the wardresses were openly sympathetic and kind, and I was told by one confidential official that they kept me only because they had orders to do so until after the great meeting at Empress Theatre, Earls Court, London, which had been arranged as a welcome home for me. The meeting was held on the Sunday night following my arrest, and the great sum of £15,000 was poured into the coffers of militancy. This included the £4,500 which had been collected during my American tour.

Several days after my release from Exeter I went openly to Paris to confer with my daughter on matters relating to the campaign about to open, returning to attend a WSPU meeting on the day before my licence expired. Nevertheless the boat train carriage in which I travelled with my doctor and nurse was invaded at Dover town by two detectives who told me to consider myself under arrest. We were making tea when the men entered, but this we immediately threw out of the window, because a hunger strike always began at the instant of arrest. We never compromised at all, but resisted from the very first moment of attack.

The reason for this uncalled for arrest at Dover was the fear on the part of the police of the bodyguard of women, just then organised for the expressed purpose of resisting attempts to arrest me. That the police, as well as the Government were afraid to risk encountering women who were not afraid to fight we had had abundant testimony. We certainly had it on this occasion, for knowing that the bodyguard was waiting at Victoria Station, the authorities had cut off all approaches to the arrival platform and the place was guarded by battalions of police. Not a passenger was permitted to leave a carriage until I had been carried across the arrival platform between a double line of police and detectives and thrown into a forty horsepower motor car, guarded within by two plain clothes men and a wardress, and without by three more policemen. Around this motor car were twelve taxicabs filled with plain clothes men, four to each vehicle, and three guarding the outside, not to mention the driver, who was also in the employ of the police department. Detectives on motor cycles were on guard at various points ready to follow any rescuing taxicab.

Arrived at Holloway I was again lifted from the car and taken to the reception room and placed on the floor in a state of great exhaustion. When the doctor came in and told me curtly to stand up I was obliged to tell him that I could not stand. I utterly refused to be examined, saying that I was resolved to make the Government assume full responsibility for my condition. 'I refuse to be examined by you or any prison doctor,' I declared, 'and I do this as a protest against my sentence, and against my being here at all. I no longer recognise a prison doctor as a medical man in the proper sense of the word. I have withdrawn my consent to be governed by the rules of prison; I refuse to recognise the authority of any prison official, and I therefore make it impossible for the Government to carry out the sentence they have imposed upon me.'

Wardresses were summoned, I was placed in an invalid chair and so carried up three flights of stairs and put into an unwarmed cell with a concrete floor. Refusing to leave the chair I was lifted out and placed on the bed, where I lay all night without removing my coat or loosening my garments. It was on a Saturday that the arrest had been made, and I was kept in prison until the following Wednesday morning. During all that time no food or water passed my lips, and I added to this the sleep strike, which means that as far as was humanly possible I refused all sleep and rest. For two nights I sat or lay on the concrete floor, resolutely refusing the oft repeated offers of medical examination. 'You are not a doctor,' I told the man. 'You are a Government torturer, and all you want to do is to satisfy yourself that I am not quite ready to die.' The doctor, a new man since my last imprisonment, flushed and looked extremely unhappy. 'I suppose you do think that,' he mumbled.

On Tuesday morning the Governor came to look at me, and no doubt I presented by that time a fairly bad appearance. At least I gathered as much from the alarmed expression of the wardress who

accompanied him. To the
simple announcement that I v.
prison and that I intended to leave ve.
or alive. I told him that from that moment .
not even rest on the concrete floor, but shou.
walk my cell until I was released or until I died
from exhaustion. All day I kept to this resolution,
pacing up and down the narrow cell, many times
stumbling and falling, until the doctor came in at
evening to tell me that I was ordered released on
the following morning. Then I loosened my gown
and lay down, absolutely spent, and fell almost
instantly into a death-like sleep. The next morning
a motor ambulance took me to the Kingsway
headquarters where a hospital room had been
arranged for my reception. The two imprisonments
in less than ten days had made terrible drafts on
my strength, and the coldness of the Holloway cell
had brought on a painful neuralgia. It was many
days before I recovered even a tithe of my usual
health.

Late in December, 1913, while I was in prison for
the second time since my return to England, a great
gala performance was given at Covent Garden, the
opera being the Jeanne d'Arc of Raymond Rôze.
The King and Queen and the entire Court were
present, and the scene was expected to be one of
unusual brilliance. Our women took advantage of
the occasion to make one of the most successful

... A box was secured
... Royal Box, and this was
... omen, beautifully gowned. On
demonstrations ... managed, without attracting the
directly ...tion, to lock and barricade the door,
...e close of the first act, as soon as the
...stra had disappeared, the women stood up,
and one of them, with the aid of a megaphone,
addressed the King. Calling attention to the
impressive scenes on the stage, the speaker told the
King that women were today fighting, as Joan of
Arc fought centuries ago, for human liberty, and
that they, like the maid of Orleans, were being
tortured and done to death, in the name of the
King, in the name of the Church, and with the full
knowledge and responsibility of established
Government. At this very hour the leader of these
fighters in the army of liberty was being held in
prison and tortured by the King's authority.

The vast audience was thrown into a panic of
excitement and horror, and amid a perfect turmoil
of cries and adjurations, the door of the box was
finally broken down and the women ejected. As
soon as they had left the house others of our women,
to the number of forty or more, who had been
sitting quietly in an upper gallery, rose to their feet
and rained suffrage literature on the heads of the
audience below. It was fully three quarters of an
hour before the excitement subsided and the singers
could go on with the opera.

The sensation caused by this direct address to Royalty inspired us to make a second attempt to arouse the King's conscience, and early in January, as soon as Parliament reassembled, we announced that I would personally lead a deputation to Buckingham Palace. The plan was welcomed with enthusiasm by our members and a very large number of women volunteered to join the deputation, which was intended to make a protest against three things—the continued disfranchisement of women; the forcible feeding and the cat and mouse torture of those who were fighting against this injustice; and the scandalous manner in which the Government, while coercing and torturing militant women, were allowing perfect freedom to the men opponents of Home Rule in Ireland, men who openly announced that they were about to carry out a policy, not merely of attacking property, but of destroying human life.

I wrote a letter to the King, conveying to him 'the respectful and loyal request of the Women's Social and Political Union that Your Majesty will give audience to a deputation of women.' The letter went on: 'The deputation desire to submit to Your Majesty in person their claim to the Parliamentary vote, which is the only protection against the grievous industrial and social wrongs that women suffer; is the symbol and guarantee of British citizenship; and means the recognition of women's equal dignity and worth, as members of our great Empire.

'The deputation will further lay before Your Majesty a complaint of the mediaeval and barbarous methods of torture whereby Your Majesty's Ministers are seeking to repress women's revolt against the deprivation of citizen rights—a revolt as noble and glorious in its spirit and purpose as any of those past struggles for liberty which are the pride of the British race.

'We have been told by the unthinking—by those who are heedless of the constitutional principles upon which is based our loyal request for an audience of Your Majesty in person—that our conversation should be with Your Majesty's Ministers.

'We repudiate this suggestion. In the first place, it would not only be repugnant to our womanly sense of dignity, but it would be absurd and futile for us to interview the very men against whom we bring the accusations of betraying the Women's Cause and torturing those who fight for that Cause.

'In the second place, we will not be referred to, and we will not recognise the authority of men who, in our eyes, have no legal or constitutional standing in the matter, because we have not been consulted as to their election to Parliament nor as to their appointment as Ministers of the Crown.'

I then cited as a precedent in support of our claim to be heard by the King in person, the case of the deputation of Irish Catholics, which, in the year 1793, was received by King George III in person.

I further said:

'Our right as women to be heard and to be aided by Your Majesty is far stronger than any such right possessed by men, because it is based upon our lack of every other constitutional means of securing the redress of our grievances. We have no power to vote for members of Parliament, and therefore for us there is no House of Commons. We have no voice in the House of Lords. But we have a King, and to him we make our appeal.

'Constitutionally speaking, we are, as voteless women, living in the time when the power of the Monarch was unlimited. In that old time, which is passed for men though not for women, men who were oppressed had recourse to the King—the source of power, of justice, and of reform.

'Precisely in the same way we now claim the right to come to the foot of the Throne and to make of the King in person our demand for the redress of the political grievance which we cannot, and will not, any longer tolerate.

'Because women are voteless, there are in our midst today sweated workers, white slaves, outraged children, and innocent mothers and their babes stricken by horrible disease. It is for the sake and in the cause of these unhappy members of our sex, that we ask of Your Majesty the audience that we are confident will be granted to us.'

It was some days before we had the answer to this letter, and in the meantime some uncommonly stirring and painful occurrences attracted the public attention.

It was about this time, February, 1914, that I undertook a series of meetings outside London, the first of which was to be held in Glasgow, in the St Andrews Hall, which holds many thousands of people. In order that I might be free on the night of the meeting, I left London unknown to the police, in a motor car. In spite of all efforts to apprehend me I succeeded in reaching Glasgow and in getting to the platform of St Andrews' where I found myself face to face with an enormous, and manifestly sympathetic audience.

As it was suspected that the police might rush the platform, plans had been made to offer resistance, and the bodyguard was present in force. My speech was one of the shortest I have ever made. I said:

'I have kept my promise, and in spite of His Majesty's Government I am here tonight. Very few people in this audience, very few people in this country, know how much of the nation's money is being spent to silence women. But the wit and ingenuity of women is overcoming the power and money of the British Government. It is well that we should have this meeting tonight, because today is a memorable day in the annals of the United Kingdom of Great Britain and Ireland. Today in the House of Commons has been witnessed the triumph of militancy—men's militancy—and tonight I hope to make it clear to the people in this meeting that if there is any distinction to be drawn at all between militancy in Ulster and the militancy of women, it is all to the advantage of the women. Our greatest task in this women's movement is to prove that we are human beings like men, and every stage of our fight is forcing home that very difficult lesson into the minds of men, and especially into the minds of politicians. I propose tonight at this political meeting to have a text. Texts are usually given from pulpits, but perhaps you will forgive me if I have a text tonight. My text is: "Equal justice for men and women, equal political justice, equal legal justice, equal industrial justice, and equal social justice." I want as clearly and briefly as I can to make it clear to you tonight that if it is justifiable to fight for common ordinary equal justice, then women have ample justification, nay, have greater justification, for revolution and rebellion, than ever men have had in the whole history of the human race. Now that is a big contention to make, but I am going to prove it. You get the proof of the political injustice—'

As I finished the word 'injustice,' a steward uttered a warning shout, there was a tramp of heavy feet, and a large body of police burst into the hall, and rushed up to the platform, drawing their truncheons as they ran. Headed by detectives from Scotland

Yard, they surged in on all sides, but as the foremost members attempted to storm the platform, they were met by a fusillade of flower-pots, tables, chairs, and other missiles. They seized the platform railing, in order to tear it down, but they found that under the decorations barbed wires were concealed. This gave them pause for a moment.

Meanwhile, more of the invading host came from other directions. The bodyguard and members of the audience vigorously repelled the attack, wielding clubs, batons, poles, planks, or anything they could seize, while the police laid about right and left with their batons, their violence being far the greater. Men and women were seen on all sides with blood streaming down their faces, and there were cries for a doctor. In the middle of the struggle, several revolver shots rang out, and the woman who was firing the revolver—which I should explain was loaded with blank cartridges only—was able to terrorise and keep at bay a whole body of police.

I had been surrounded by members of the bodyguard, who hurried me towards the stairs from the platform. The police, however, overtook us, and in spite of the resistance of the bodyguard, they seized me and dragged me down the narrow stair at the back of the hall. There a cab was waiting. I was pushed violently into it, and thrown on the floor, the seats being occupied by as many constables as could crowd inside.

The meeting was left in a state of tremendous turmoil, and the people of Glasgow who were present expressed their sense of outrage at the behaviour of the police, who, acting under the Government's instructions, had so disgraced the city. General Drummond, who was present on the platform, took hold of the situation and delivered a rousing speech, in which she exhorted the audience to make the Government feel the force of their indignation.

I was kept in the Glasgow police-cells all night, and the next morning was taken, a hunger and thirst striking prisoner, to Holloway, where I remained for five memorable days. This was the seventh attempt the Government had made to make me serve a three years' term of penal servitude on a conspiracy charge, in connection with the blowing up of Mr Lloyd-George's country house. In the eleven and a half months since I had received that sentence I had spent just thirty days in prison. On March 14th I was again released, still suffering severely, not only from the hunger and thirst strike, but from injuries received at the time of my brutal arrest in Glasgow.

The answer to that arrest had been swift and strong. In Bristol, the scene of great riots and destruction when men were fighting for votes, a large timber-yard was burnt. In Scotland a mansion was destroyed by fire. A milder protest consisted of a raid upon the house of the Home

Secretary, in the course of which eighteen windows were broken.

The greatest and most startling of all protests hitherto made was the attack at this time on the Rokeby 'Venus' in the National Gallery. Mary Richardson, the young woman who carried out this protest, is possessed of a very fine artistic sense, and nothing but the most compelling sense of duty would have moved her to the deed. Miss Richardson being placed on trial, made a moving address to the court, in the course of which she said that her act was premeditated, and that she had thought it over very seriously before it was undertaken. She added: 'I have been a student of art, and I suppose care as much for art as any one who was in the gallery when I made my protest. But I care more for justice than I do for art, and I firmly believe than when a nation shuts its eyes to justice, and prefers to have women who are fighting for justice ill-treated, mal-treated, and tortured, that such action as mine should be understandable; I don't say excusable, but it should be understood.

'I should like to point out that the outrage which the Government has committed upon Mrs Pankhurst is an ultimatum of outrages. It is murder, slow murder, and premeditated murder. That is how I have looked at it. . . .

'How you can hold women up to ridicule and contempt, and put them in prison, and yet say nothing to the Government for murdering people, I cannot understand . . .

'The fact is that the nation is either dead or asleep. In my opinion there is undoubted evidence that the nation is dead, because women have knocked in vain at the door of administrators, archbishops, and even the King himself. The Government have closed all doors to us. And remember this—a state of death in a nation, as well as in an individual, leads to one thing, and that is dissolution. I do not hesitate to say that if the men of the country do not at this eleventh hour put their hand out and save Mrs Pankhurst, before a few more years are passed they will stretch out their hand in vain to save the Empire.'

In sentencing Miss Richardson to six months' imprisonment the Magistrate said regretfully that if she had smashed a window instead of an art treasure he could have given her a maximum sentence of eighteen months, which illustrates, I think, one more queer anomaly of English law.

A few weeks later another famous painting, the Sargent portrait of Henry James, was attacked by a Suffragette, who, like Miss Richardson, was sent through the farce of a trial and a prison sentence which she did not serve. By this time practically all the picture galleries and other public galleries and museums had been closed to the public. The Suffragettes had succeeded in large measure in making England unattractive to tourists, and hence unprofitable to the world of business. As we had anticipated, the reaction against the Liberal Government began to manifest itself. Questions were asked daily, in the press, in the House of Commons, everywhere, as to the responsibility of the Government in the Suffragette activities. People began to place that responsibility where it belonged, at the doors of the Government, rather than at our own.

I had appointed May 21st for the deputation, in spite of the fact that the King had, through his Ministers, refused to receive us. Replying to this I had written, again directly to the King, that we utterly denied the constitutional right of Ministers, who not being elected by women were not responsible to them, to stand between ourselves and the Throne, and to prevent us from having an audience of His Majesty. I declared further that we would, on the date announced, present ourselves at the gates of Buckingham Palace to demand an interview.

Following the despatch of this letter my life was made as uncomfortable and as insecure as the Government, through their police department, could contrive. I was not allowed to make a public appearance, but I addressed several huge meetings from the balcony of houses where I had taken refuge. These were all publicly announced, and each time the police, mingling with crowds, made strenuous efforts to arrest me. By strategy, and through the valiant efforts of the bodyguard, I was able each time to make my speech and afterwards to escape from the house. All of these occasions were marked by fierce opposition from the police and splendid courage and resistance on the part of the women.

The deputation to the King was, of course, marked by the Government as an occasion on which I could be arrested, and when, on the day appointed, I led the great deputation of women to the gates of Buckingham Palace, an army of several thousand police were sent out against us. The conduct of the police showed plainly that they had been instructed to repeat the tactics of Black Friday, described in an earlier chapter. Indeed, the violence, brutality and insult of Black Friday were excelled on this day, and at the gates of the King of England. I myself did not suffer so greatly as others, because I had advanced towards the Palace unnoticed by the police, who were looking for me at a more distant point. When I arrived at the gates I was recognised by an Inspector, who at once seized me bodily, and conveyed me to Holloway.

Before the deputation had gone forth, I had made a short speech to them, warning them of what might happen, and my final message was: 'Whatever happens, do not turn back.' They did not, and in spite of all the violence inflicted upon them, they went forward, resolved, so long as they were free, not to give up the attempt to reach the

Palace. Many arrests were made, and of those arrested many were sent to prison. Although for the majority, this was the first imprisonment, these brave women adopted the hunger strike, and passed seven or eight days without food and water before they were released, weak and ill as may be supposed.

But now unmistakable signs began to appear that our long and bitter struggle was drawing to a close. The last resort of the Government of inciting the street mobs against us had been little successful, and we could see in the temper of the public abundant hope that the reaction against the Government, long hoped for by us, had actually begun.

Every day of the militant movement was so extraordinarily full of events and changes that it is difficult to choose a point at which this narrative should be brought to a close. I think, however, that an account of a recent debate which took place in the House of Commons will give the reader the best idea of the complete breakdown of the Government in their effort to crush the women's fight for liberty.

On June 11th, when the House of Commons had gone into a Committee of Supply, Lord Robert Cecil moved a reduction of one hundred pounds on the Home Office vote, thus precipitating a discussion of militancy. Lord Robert said that he had read with some surprise that the Government were not dissatisfied with the measures which they had taken to deal with the violent suffragists, and he added with some asperity that the Government took a much more sanguine view of the matter than anybody else in the United Kingdom. The House, Lord Robert went on to declare, would not be in a position to deal with the case satisfactorily unless they realised the devotion of the followers to their leaders, who were almost fully responsible for what was going on. Ministerial cheers greeted this utterance, but they ceased suddenly when the speaker went on to say that these leaders could never have induced their followers to enter upon a career of crime but for the serious mistakes which had been made over and over again by the Government. Among these mistakes Lord Robert cited the shameful treatment of the women on Black Friday, the policy of forcible feeding and the scandal of the different treatment accorded Lady Constance Lytton and 'Jane Warton.' There were Opposition cheers at this, and they were again raised when Lord Robert deplored the terrible waste of energy, and 'admirable material' involved in the militant movement. Although Lord Robert Cecil deemed it unjust as well as futile for suffragist members to withhold their support from the woman suffrage movement on account of militancy he himself was in favor of deportation for Suffragettes. At this there were cries of 'Where to?' and 'Ulster!'

Mr McKenna replied by first calling attention to the fact that in the militant movement they had a phenomenon 'absolutely without precedent in our history.' Women in numbers were committing crimes, beginning with window-breaking, and proceeding to arson, not with the motives of ordinary criminals, but with the intention of advertising a political cause and of forcing the public to grant their demands. Mr McKenna continuing said:

'The number of women who commit crimes of that kind is extremely small, but the number of those who sympathise with them is extremely large. One of the difficulties which the police have in detecting this form of crime and in bringing home the offence to the criminal is that the criminals find so many sympathisers among the well-to-do and thoroughly respectable classes that the ordinary administration of the law is rendered comparatively impossible.'

Mr McKenna went on to say that he realised fully the growing sense of indignation against the militant suffragists and he added, 'Their one hope is, rightly or wrongly, that the well advertised indignation of the public will recoil on the head of the Government.'

'And so it will,' interpolated a voice.

'My honourable friend,' replied Mr McKenna, 'says so it will. I believe that he is mistaken.' But he gave no reasons for so believing. Referring to what he called the 'recent grave rudenesses which have been committed against the King,' Mr McKenna said: 'It is true that all subjects have the right of petitioning His Majesty, providing the petition is couched in respectful terms, but there is no right on the part of the subjects generally to personal audience for the purpose of the presentation of the petition or otherwise. It is the duty of the Home Secretary to present all such petitions to the King, and further to advise His Majesty what action should be taken. It was therefore ridiculous for any suffragist to assert that there had been any breach of constitutional propriety on the part of the King in refusing, on the advice of the Home Secretary to receive the deputation.'

Also, said Mr McKenna, in view of the fact that the petition for an audience was sent by a person under sentence of penal servitude—myself—it was the plain duty of the Home Secretary to advise the King not to grant it. He referred to the incident, he said, only because it was illustrative of the militants' methods of advertising their cause. He gave them credit, he was bound to say, for a certain degree of intelligence in adopting their methods. 'No action has been so fruitful of advertisement as the recent absurdities which they have perpetrated in relation to the King.'

Coming at last to the constructive part of his speech Mr McKenna told the House of Commons that the Government had one last resort, which was to take legal proceedings against subscribers to the funds of the WSPU. The funds of the society, he said, were undoubtedly beyond the arm of the British law. But the Government were in hopes of stopping future subscriptions. 'We are now not without hope,' he concluded, 'that we have evidence which will enable us to proceed against the subscribers' (loud cheers) 'in civil action, and if we succeed the subscribers will become personally liable for all the damage done.' (Cheers.) 'It is a question of evidence. . . . I have further directed that the question should be considered whether the subscribers could not be proceeded against criminally as well as by civil action.' (Cheers.) 'We have only been able to obtain this evidence by our now not infrequent raids upon the offices, and such property as we can get at of the society. . . . A year ago a raid was made on the offices of the society, but we obtained no such evidence. If we succeed in making the subscribers personally responsible individually for the whole damage done I have no doubt that the insurance companies will quickly follow the example set them by the Government, and in turn bring actions to recover the cost which has been thrown upon them. If that is done I have no doubt the days of militancy are over.

'The militants live only by the subscriptions of rich women' (cheers) 'who themselves enjoy all the advantages of wealth secured for them by the labour of others' (cheers) 'and use their wealth against the interests of society, paying their unfortunate victims to undergo all the horrors of a hunger and thirst strike in the commission of a crime. Whatever feelings we may have against the wretched women who for 30s. and £2 a week go about the country burning and destroying, what must our feelings be for the women who give their money to induce the perpetration of these crimes and leave their sisters to undergo the punishment while they live in luxury?' (Cheers.) 'If we can succeed against them we will spare no pains. If the action is successful in the total destruction of the means of revenue of the Women's Social and Political Union I think we shall see the last of the power of Mrs Pankhurst and her friends.' (Cheers.)

In the general debate which followed the Government were obliged to listen to very severe criticisms of their past and present policy towards the militant women. Mr Keir Hardie said in part:

'We may not today discuss the question of the franchise, but surely it was possible for the Home Secretary, without any transgression on the rules of the House, to have held out just a ray of hope for the future as to the intentions of the Government in regard to this most urgent question. On that point, may I say that I am not one of those who believe that a right thing should be withheld because some of the advocates of it resort to weapons of which we do not approve. That note has been sounded more than once, and if it be true, and it is true, that a section of the public outside are strongly opposed to this conduct, it is equally true that the bulk of the people look with a very calm and indifferent eye upon what is happening so long as the vote is withheld from women.'

Mr Hardie concluded by regretting that the House, instead of discussing Woman Suffrage, was discussing methods of penalising militant women.

Mr Rupert Gwynne said: 'Nobody is in a more ridiculous position than the members on the Treasury Bench. They cannot address a meeting, or go to a railway station, or even get into a taxicab, without having detectives with them. Even if they like it, we, the public do not, because we have to pay for it. It is not worth the expense that it costs to have a detective staff following Cabinet Ministers wherever they go, whether in a private or a public capacity.

'Further,' said Mr Gwynne, 'if the Home Secretary is correct in saying that these women are prepared to die, and invite death, in order to advertise their devotion to their cause, does he really think they are going to mind if their funds are attached?'

Another friend of the suffragists, Mr Wedgwood said: 'We are dealing with a problem which is a very serious one indeed. To my mind, when you find a large body of public opinion, and a large number of people capable of going to these lengths, there is only one thing for a respectable House of

Commons to do, and that is to consider very closely and clearly whether the complaints of those who complain are or are not justified. We are not justified in acting in panic. What it is our duty to do is to consider the rights and wrongs of these people who have acted in this way. I attribute myself no value to the vote, but I do think that when we seriously consider the question of Woman Suffrage, which has not been done by this House up to the present, we should remember that when you see people capable of this amount of self-sacrifice, that the one duty of the House of Commons is not to stamp the iron heel upon them, but to see how far their cause is just, and to act according to justice.'

When such a debate as this was possible in the House of Commons, it must be plain to every disinterested reader that militancy never set the cause of suffrage back, but on the contrary, set it forward at least half a century. When I remember how that same House of Commons, a few years ago, treated the mention of woman suffrage with scorn and contempt, how they permitted the most insulting things to be said of the women who were begging for their political freedom, how, with indecent laughter and coarse jokes they allowed suffrage bills to be talked out, I cannot but marvel at the change our militancy so quickly brought about. Mr McKenna's speech was in itself a token of the complete surrender of the Government.

Of course the promise of the Home Secretary that subscribers to our funds should, if possible, be held legally responsible for damage done to private property by the Suffragettes, was never meant to be adhered to. It was, in fact, a perfectly absurd promise, and I think that very few members of Parliament were deceived by it. Our subscribers can always remain anonymous if they choose, and if it should ever be possible to attack them for our deeds, they would naturally take refuge behind that privilege.

Our battles are practically over, we confidently believe. For the present at least our arms are grounded, for directly the threat of foreign war descended on our nation we declared a complete truce from militancy. What will come out of this European war—so terrible in its effects on the women who had no voice in averting it—so baneful in the suffering it must necessarily bring on innocent children—no human being can calculate. But one thing is reasonably certain, and that is that the Cabinet changes which will necessarily result from warfare will make future militancy on the part of women unnecessary. No future Government will repeat the mistakes and the brutality of the Asquith Ministry. None will be willing to undertake the impossible task of crushing or even delaying the march of women towards their rightful heritage of political liberty and social and industrial freedom.

THE END

VINTAGE CLASSICS

penguin.co.uk/vintage-classics